# Praise for *Meta-Leadership*

"Constance Dierickx has managed to write the ultimate book on thinking, leading, and making good decisions. In *Meta-Leadership*, she blends the scientific insights of a Dan Ariely, the wisdom and perspective of a Marcus Aurelius, and the business knowledge of a Jim Collins. It's the book that I wish I had written, and I couldn't endorse it more strongly."

**DANNY INY**, founder/CEO of Mirasee and author of *Leveraged Learning*

"A groundbreaking, evidence-driven book that helps leaders evaluate and improve their own thinking, emotions, and behaviors—the three elements that combine into what Constance Dierickx calls 'meta-leadership.' Unfortunately, leaders are often told they should go with their gut and trust their intuition. Doing so often causes disastrous decisions, because leaders don't question the distortions in their intuitive thinking, emotions, and behaviors. With the help of this book, leaders will make much wiser and more profitable decisions, because they will see reality clearly and avoid black-and-white thinking. A winner!"

**GLEB TSIPURSKY**, PhD, bestselling author of *Never Go With Your Gut*

"Constance Dierickx has produced an insightful, pragmatic book examining the human tendency to use black-and-white thinking, even when we shouldn't. *Meta-Leadership* shows anyone who is or aspires to be a leader how to improve, zeroing in on the personal, social, and situational forces that affect how we think, decide, and act. Drawing on research and illuminated by memorable examples, this book shines a needed light on leadership from the inside out."

**DORIE CLARK**, *Wall Street Journal*–bestselling author of *The Long Game* and executive education faculty at Duke University Fuqua School of Business

"Meta-leadership is the art of seeing a situation clearly—and without distortion—so you can make the strongest, most sound executive decisions possible. For today's leaders, this practice is indispensable. Author and advisor Constance Dierickx should be given a standing ovation for her pioneering work on the subject."

**MARK LEVY,** CEO of Levy Innovation and creator of Your Big Sexy Idea

"In *Meta-Leadership*, Constance Dierickx explains that being a wise leader—not just a smart or knowledgeable one—requires the ability to push past simplistic dichotomies by relying on a more complex understanding of our thoughts, feelings, and behaviors. Her own wisdom shines through from start to finish as she beautifully weaves together her knowledge as a PhD psychologist, her decades of experience as an executive consultant, and her ability to synthesize research into compelling prose."

**JAMES DETERT,** PhD, John L. Colley Professor at Darden School of Business, University of Virginia, and author of *Choosing Courage*

"Great leaders think differently. In the face of massive and sometimes contradictory information, they avoid the deadly trap of dichotomous thinking. In *Meta-Leadership*, Constance Dierickx shows us how great leaders combine intellect and emotion, and information with insight. Rigorous research illuminated by stories of admirable, and some not-so-great, leaders make *Meta-Leadership* an essential read for leaders and those who aspire to lead with excellence."

**FRANCES X. FREI,** UPS Foundation Professor of Service Management at Harvard Business School and coauthor of *Uncommon Service*

"A powerful and comprehensive guide to seeing past distortions to make great decisions! Constance Dierickx's expert knowledge combines with actionable advice for a must-read book for every leader."

**DR. MARSHALL GOLDSMITH,** Thinkers50 #1 executive coach and *New York Times*–bestselling author of *The Earned Life*

# META LEADER-SHIP

HOW TO SEE WHAT

OTHERS DON'T AND MAKE

GREAT DECISIONS

CONSTANCE DIERICKX PhD

# META LEADER-SHIP

Some names and identifying details have been changed
to protect the privacy of individuals.

Cataloguing in publication information is available
from Library and Archives Canada.
ISBN 978-1-77458-216-9 (hardcover)
ISBN 978-1-77458-217-6 (ebook)
ISBN 978-1-77458-338-8 (audiobook)

Page Two
pagetwo.com

Edited by Kendra Ward
Copyedited by Jenny Govier
Proofread by Alison Strobel
Jacket and interior design by Peter Cocking
Indexed by Stephen Ullstrom
Printed and bound in Canada by Friesens
Distributed in Canada by Raincoast Books
Distributed in the US and internationally by Macmillan

23  24  25  26  27    5  4  3  2  1

constancedierickx.com

*To Michael*

# Contents

# Introduction

FRIDAY, JUNE 17, began as a sunny, if slightly windy, day along the Scottish coast of the North Sea. Visitors leaned into the wind, fearing they might be blown sideways, or worse. In contrast, residents carried on as if it were an ordinary day, utterly unworthy of comment. Stone houses on narrow streets had open windows with curtains batting like pale eyelashes, while overhead sea birds, barely flapping their wings, moved with the wind currents. Returning to their cruise ship, visitors told stories of ancient churches, the kindness of the locals, and their surprise at the strong wind and cold temperature.

Alfred Korzybski, a scientist and philosopher, said, "A map is not the territory," and this experience was, for me, a perfect embodiment of this idea.[1] I had read about the places we would visit, and Scottish born-and-raised friends had warned me about the cold, rain, and wind. I had gone so far as to purchase a new Barbour coat, complete with hood. The coat, as terrific as it was, could not shield me from the weather.

On the bridge, the ship's captain was surveying the territory with entirely different methods—navigation tools and weather reports. Passengers, including me, were preoccupied by what we could see, but the captain was busy predicting. He knew a storm was headed toward the north of Scotland—the Orkney and Shetland islands—exactly where the ship was headed and precisely where my husband and I had been planning (for an embarrassingly long time) to visit. I was focused on my own experience, on the present and recent past, but the captain was concerned with a larger and more intricate landscape, which would soon become obvious.

At 4:30 p.m., during the daily teatime (complete with scones and other delights that ought to have made dinner unnecessary, but didn't), the captain made an announcement. We would be going to neither the Orkney Islands nor the Shetlands. Instead, we would spend the next two days hanging out in the North Sea, well south of the weather that could imperil us. As soon as the announcement was made, passengers began expressing their opinions about what was happening, and they ran the full gamut from angry to grateful. I felt disappointment, then immediately short-circuited that feeling with the same thought I have when a flight I'm on is diverted or changes trajectory unexpectedly, at an angle not usual for commercial travel. My thought is always that the person making the decision is the best person to make it. Why? Because the person deciding has an array of educational and training experiences and has performed in situations in which the criteria for what is good enough is clear.

A great pilot is a leader who must think holistically and intentionally if they are to avoid the invisible traps that can trip up even smart and experienced people. The ship's captain on June 17 had to consider not only the weather and what the ship could safely navigate, but also how passengers might react to being aboard in high winds and waves that would cause the ship to feel unstable.

The captain delivered a calm, clear, and organized message, referring to his most important duty: ensuring the safety of the ship and its passengers. Next, he described the conditions to the north and how they were expected to evolve. Finally, he informed us of the risk of attempting to sail into these conditions and stated his decision and the plan.

I listened with the concern of a passenger and the experience of a consultant who has worked with hundreds of leaders. I felt confident in this captain and admired his skill as a leader. It is people like him, and there are many, who can think above and beyond, direct their emotion in the most helpful way, and act with confidence that is credible, who exemplify meta-leadership.

## Meta-Leadership Is Essential

Leaders today face greater challenges than at any other time in history. They must make decisions in a complex environment that changes with lightning speed and in which risks are often obscured. A massive amount of input comes from advisors, media, and sometimes gossip—distortions are inevitable. Sometimes the sheer volume and variety of information cause misinterpretations, and other times, people delivering information are willfully misleading. Those who try to influence a leader may shape their message with such skill as to steer the leader's attention, encourage them to accept a particular version of the truth, and take the wrong actions. Leaders also have their own tendencies of thinking that are influenced by cognitive biases, beliefs, and experiences that interfere with their ability to see reality. Yet, even with conscious and unconscious, unwitting and willful distortion, leaders must make decisions that affect their teams, the organization, and perhaps even the world.

How can you make good leadership decisions when awash with so much good information and so much wrong information? It takes what I call meta-leadership, the ability to step back from all the noise and distortion and see things as they truly are. When you master the art of meta-leadership, you have a huge competitive advantage over those who make decisions based on distortion—and whose confidence remains intact even as they stand on shaky ground. All the time, millions, if not billions, of dollars are committed to ill-advised strategic moves by leaders who feel confident without good reason.

The art of meta-leadership allows you to be far better than competitors at seeing what is true and what isn't. Your decisions will be more accurate, you will be justifiably confident, and your competitors won't know what hit them.

## We Need to Avoid This Trap

Information gets distorted in many ways. In *Meta-Leadership: How to See What Others Don't and Make Great Decisions*, I examine a cognitive trap so prevalent people rarely take note of it: dichotomous thinking, or thinking in black and white, as though with any choice there is a clear, definitive, correct approach and an equally clear wrong one.

Because the world is more connected than at any time in history, it is more complex. Although we have enormous amounts of data and input, we can't trust that it is all accurate. The first cognitive task is attention: To what do we attend? The second is meaning: What does this thing, person, or idea mean? Where does this input fit, or does it? Humans have a tremendous capacity to sort with little effort or awareness, and this is both a gift and a trap. When we attend to familiar people and situations, the risk of mistakes is lower because we use experience and patterns within those experiences to guide our decisions, and we do so with little effort. However, when something is unfamiliar, or perhaps dangerous, it is riskier to rely on quick, black-and-white thinking, which tends to amplify similarities and discount differences that, although subtle, may be important.

# The art of meta-leadership allows you to be far better than competitors at seeing what is true and what isn't.

—————

I first noticed the trap of dichotomous thinking decades ago when I was a stockbroker. My clients were all smart people, but they were often swayed by the most irrelevant factors—what their friends advised, where they were employed, and myths about the value of stock splits or reliable dividend payments and the like. Their emotions were far more influential in their decision-making than they would admit.

The most stubborn clients were physicians, accountants, and professors, all of whom trusted their superior knowledge and intellect, regardless of their expertise in securities. They were shocked when they suffered losses, but not astonished enough to examine their thinking. I was haunted by how many intelligent, highly skilled, critically thinking people made risky decisions about their money but didn't realize it, no matter my efforts. In particular, I was surprised by people who were stuck in very concrete thinking such as, "Stocks are bad; people should only buy US Treasury bonds," or, "I will only consider no-load mutual funds; the others are a rip-off." These are oversimplified ways of thinking, but they have appeal because when people have strong beliefs, decisions can be made faster and with less effort.

Unable to let go of my quandary and finding my colleagues had no explanations to offer for my clients' seemingly incongruent behavior, I dug around in books, first in decision science, then in psychology. I saw that both had something to offer. But decision scientists were mainly hanging on to the idea that people are rational actors, and psychologists were too suspicious of investing to take a genuine interest.

Then the stock market crashed.

On Monday, October 19, 1987, the Dow Jones suffered the most significant percentage loss of all time, 22.6 percent. At the time of writing, the same percentage drop would equate to nearly 8,000 points—a panic-inducing loss for sure. In the chaos that ensued, I observed how different people responded. Some were sanguine and looked to the larger context and history; these people did nothing with their investments, and I was among them. However, some people panicked and made terrible, life-altering decisions like selling all their investments at the worst possible time. Still others blamed their advisors, brokers, and even spouses for losses that, unless investments were sold, were paper losses only. Seeing how people responded ignited my desire to understand the world's best thinkers and leaders and what made them different, especially in a crisis.

In the aftermath of the crash, it became clear that I was in the wrong job, so I quit and went back to school. I found a place where asking questions was not a sign of weakness. If a professor didn't know an answer but thought my question was interesting, they suggested I investigate. Finally, I was on the right path.

Over the next twenty-five years, I advised more than forty boards and hundreds of leaders at the top of companies in over twenty-five industries, in more than thirty countries, on five continents. I have seen leaders try various tactics to improve leadership, teamwork, and results, with varying degrees of success and sometimes complete failure. One leader who consulted me after a failed attempt to make a major change said, "We spent a million dollars and got a pep rally." That's what happens when you take shortcuts, jump on bandwagons, and use rigid methods.

The best leaders I know, and some I have studied at a distance, adopt the strategy of meta-leadership—a way of thinking, using emotion, and making decisions so that distortions, including dichotomies, have less sway and reality takes precedence.

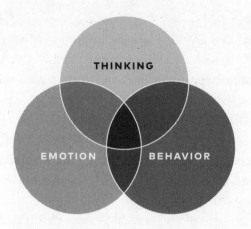

DIMENSIONS OF META-LEADERSHIP

## Studying Our Own Leadership

The origin of "meta" is Greek, and it means "beyond"; for instance, meta-physics is the science of what is beyond the physical. The term "meta" has been adapted in common use to refer to something above the thing itself. "Meta-analysis" is a good example. It is analysis of data from multiple sources or studies that also use analysis. "Meta-cognition" means thinking about thinking.

"Meta-leadership" refers to studying one's own leadership, using a broad and holistic point of view rather than a set of skills. Of course, great leaders possess knowledge and skill, but they are also very observant and discerning, especially about what or who may distort reality. They eschew the notion that they are infallible. Good leaders become great in part because they recognize that their own thinking, emotions, and habits of behavior can be a source of error. They may appear humble, but their humility is the result of discipline and respect for reality. Conversely, the most vulnerable leaders are unaware of the human tendency to distort reality or, worse, assume they are above it. They are overconfident in their decision-making process and use it in a mechanical fashion, making it even more difficult to see clearly.

In my years of advising senior leaders who collectively influence the lives of millions of people, I have observed that those who use meta-leadership as a strategy are more successful. Meta-leaders create value for customers, employees, shareholders, and communities—perhaps even the global community. They aren't incrementalists, but neither are they detached from reality, though it may appear so to some.

Meta-leadership is conceptual and, even for those intrigued by it, not easy to use pragmatically without exploring its dimensions: thinking, emotion, and behavior. While these are easily recognizable aspects of human beings—we think, feel, and act—most of us need specific examples and some way to tie them to the ideas. I think of it as cognitive scaffolding, a way to move from details to a concept and back again, logically. In meta-leadership, the particular scaffolding I chose is made up of three sections: thinking, emotion, and behavior. These are explored via several dichotomies, in particular the following:

- Certain and uncertain
- Rational and irrational
- Strategic and tactical
- Analytical and creative
- Courageous and cowardly
- Independent and dependent
- Analysis and synthesis
- Now and later
- Knowledgeable and wise

Each pair has its own chapter in this book, with examples of great and not-so-great leadership.

## Meta-Leadership Transformed Georgia State University

Atlanta, Georgia, is home to Georgia State University (GSU), a public institution that began as an urban business school but has become a major research university. It is nicknamed "the concrete campus," and it would be an understatement to say that the campus I saw on my visit as a prospective graduate student in psychology was neither beautiful nor inviting. Despite the lack of aesthetic appeal, I was attracted to the breadth of research being done at GSU.

Like most graduate students, I took on teaching assistant jobs, which showed me firsthand the problem plaguing GSU—retention. Undergraduates, transitioning from high school to a university that at the time had more than 30,000 students and no dorms, had to deal with the reality of an urban campus—traffic, crowds, confusing streets (I joke that the streets are former goat paths, now paved), and parking problems that were a constant source of frustration. Adding to the challenges faced by students at all levels were administrative functions that were hard to navigate, offices that were open or closed seemingly by whim, and staff whose attitudes varied from helpful and kind to dismissive and rude. My classmates and I, undeterred, shared information with each other—when were the best times to go to which office, who was most helpful, and how to get assistance from the department secretary. (We nicknamed her the troll under the bridge, which might have been a little ungenerous, if it weren't for the fact that she displayed an astounding lack of empathy and seemed to take pleasure in creating obstacles in front of barriers to whatever administrative hoops we needed to jump through.) The bureaucracy was annoying for my classmates and me, but it could be a much bigger impediment for some undergraduates. Undergraduate students who were the first in the family to attend college were at a particular disadvantage, in part because their parents may not have been able to help, not because they didn't want to, but because they may not have known how.

I haven't even mentioned coursework yet. For some students, the expectations came as a shock and felt unfair. The surprise was acute for students who had done well in high school and been encouraged to attend college but didn't have the advantage of attending a good high school. It's easy to blame individuals for poor performance, and sometimes it's justified. But for some students, an insufficient showing wasn't about a lack of dedication or hard work. Rather, they came from disadvantaged circumstances, a corollary of which can be lower SAT scores.

When I was a teaching assistant, we believed that SAT scores were the best predictor of college success. This truism was rarely questioned, but that changed when GSU, with the insight and challenge of Dr. Timothy Renick, began to ask if the long-held belief in the predictive value of SAT scores was true at all, or if it was partly true but far from the whole story.

## Intentional Adaptation

Renick joined the GSU faculty in 1986, fresh from completing his PhD at Princeton. Hired to start a department of religion, he began as the only faculty member of the department and needed to develop the courses and teach all of them himself. Renick dug into the challenge and over the next five years hired three additional faculty and proposed a BA degree, all while distinguishing himself as an excellent teacher. The department grew and classes filled quickly, but Renick didn't confine his work to the classroom. He taught groups in the Atlanta community, as well as directing students in independent study, honors theses, and master's theses. A dedicated teacher, he writes, "If a professor is to challenge, he or she also must encourage."[2]

Renick's commitment to teaching is motivated by a desire to challenge students and also by a sharp understanding of the transformative power of a college education, which increases the likelihood that a person will have greater income. Further, college graduates are likely to enjoy a longer life and better healthcare than those who do not graduate—and so will their children.[3] Higher education not only transforms the lives of college graduates and their families, but it can also change a family for generations.

Currently, Renick heads the National Institute for Student Success. There he and his team constantly improve how the university interacts with students. The story of the student success program at GSU and the creation of the National Institute for Student Success is told in Andrew Gumbel's book *Won't Lose This Dream*.[4] Gumbel beautifully describes Renick's determination, compassion, and preference for facts no matter how they may contradict common knowledge. Those qualities make him a worthy example of meta-leadership, even while Renick may seem an unlikely character to be the architect of an exceptional transformation of undergraduate education outcomes, radically improving graduation rates of students from underserved backgrounds at a behemoth institution like GSU.

Meta-leadership requires both a willingness and an ability to alter one's altitude, standing back at times and zooming in at others, getting stuck in neither perspective by default. Such flexibility requires intentional adaptation rather than reaction to external forces.

In the case of GSU, the forces that made success more difficult for students from underserved backgrounds weren't only external to the university, they were within the very structure and processes of school itself. For example, academic leaders had long believed in their right to maintain their own databases, each in their own way. They resisted using a common data set for all students, which prevented university-wide analysis that was needed to track students and create effective interventions broadly. Renick and his colleagues were determined to figure out the issue using facts, some of which challenged long-held beliefs and made faculty and administrators uncomfortable, if not angry. However, once people began to believe in the possibilities, the proverbial flywheel began to turn. Renick says that getting people to believe in the change he envisioned was one of the hardest parts of the transformation. He rightly says, "Bureaucracy deadens enthusiasm."[5] When the benefits were clearly laid out, university leaders including Mark Becker, then the president of GSU, could see the value to students *and* the school. Students dropping out was not just a burden for the individuals, but it meant churn in the population and loss of revenue from tuition, not to mention damage to GSU's reputation.

GSU's impressive graduation rate of students from underserved backgrounds—equal to or greater than the overall student population—is stunning. Achieving it took work on multiple fronts, simultaneously, deliberately avoiding the temptation to use dichotomous thinking to look for a silver bullet.

## Engaging Data *and* Story

None of these changes at GSU happened until Renick took on the challenge and painted a vision that shattered the dichotomous thinking that "some students were headed for success and some were doomed to failure." One way he did this was by bringing data and story together.

Accurate data about students was, and is, critical to the ability of GSU to improve student experience and retention rates. Gathering the right information on thousands of students took a coordinated effort, technology, and insight to generate accurate predictions. A chatbot, in this case a caricature of the GSU mascot (a panther named Pounce), ultimately enabled students to access information any day, any time, and the data from these interactions could be analyzed by computers. But what then? Using predictive analytics, the system at GSU generates alerts that go directly to advisors to let them know when a student needs help. More than 800 different types of alerts give advisors specific information about students and allow them to reach out proactively. Students also receive messages from Pounce reminding them about enrollment tasks and suggesting relevant support programs for improving grades or managing difficult personal issues. No judgment, just information. A university now serving more than 52,000 students needs the right number of advisors with the right skills and temperament who also receive the right support. Before GSU transformed its student outcomes, advisors were each responsible for 1,100 students. That number is now 300, and the same systems that make student's lives better also make the advising role more rewarding.

The technology alone would not have been enough to generate the improvements at GSU. Renick estimates that technology contributed about 10 percent of the improvement. The other 90 percent was his leadership team. His impassioned belief in the university's ability to facilitate rather than dare students to succeed was important, but so too were cold hard facts. Renick marries deeply moving stories of students with the facts about the value to society of making success in college possible for more students who are willing. This is meta-leadership.

Observing talented leaders who never cease to learn and evolve, who have the courage that matches their talent while remaining keenly aware of their fallibility, led me to develop the term "meta-leadership." Meta-leaders, no matter how tactical they may act at times, are relentlessly driven by strategic purpose. They are the ultimate ship captains who lead, teach, learn, love what they do, and care deeply about people.

# PART I

# THINKING ABOUT THINKING

**W**HAT IS BETTER than examining failures to discover what caused them? Looking for the causes of the causes: the habits of mind and behavior, processes both documented and undocumented, interpersonal entanglements, expectations, and fears. Postmortems and case studies can illuminate causes such as poor data, bad management, inadequate tools, lack of training, and so on, but those are merely the manifestations of an underlying cause. Great leaders look at how such limitations came to be and what prevents improvement because they understand that dysfunctional dynamics will appear again and again, but in what may be deceptively distinct costumes. Seeing the underlying cause requires more than awareness of what one thinks. It requires the willingness to examine how one thinks and what influences are at play.

When leaders understand thinking about thinking, they begin to see how to embed it in virtually everything they do, thus providing a model for others. Great leaders also quickly spot substitutions for great thinking, including mountains of data, analysis, invalid measures, and the like, which can be easily revealed with simple questions, such as, "How did we decide to use that metric?" or, "Who decided?"

Leaders who prioritize time to think are more likely to see what is really going on and sidestep dichotomies that lead to myriad invisible decision traps.

1

# A Certain Discomfort with Uncertainty

People hurl a tremendous amount of
information at leaders. Some is true and accurate,
some is intentionally distorted or simply
untrue, and some is contradictory. Great leaders
use meta-cognition (thinking about thinking)
to sort reality from distortion.

**M**ARK, THE CEO of a public company, was an imposing man who never minced words. He sat across the boardroom table from me, flipping pages and looking like a heavyweight fighter wearing a well-tailored suit to disguise himself as a refined leader. In front of him was my report, an assessment of a candidate for the head of sales in a $14 billion global company. Mark looked like he might explode. Visibly irritated, he was flushed and his hand was tightly wrapped around his elegant Montblanc pen in a vain attempt to thwart his anger. Finally, he exploded at me: "I can't give your report to my board. You didn't give me what I need to hire the guy!" At that moment I realized that Mark wanted me to talk only about all the reasons the candidate was perfect for the job. But he wasn't. No one is perfect for a particular role. Mark feared that my nuanced description of the person he had selected would give the board room to disagree with his decision.

Mark was in the grip of uncertainty, a characteristic that many leaders are loath to display. Although most boards want a CEO who is open-minded, thoughtful, and deliberate, too often they reward decisiveness even at the expense of accuracy, often unwittingly. Leaders who are sure of themselves and their decisions fit the hero archetype that lives in our unconscious. Believing that someone is a great leader is easier if they look and act the part, including being decisive. A leader who shows up in the boardroom or at a town hall meeting and is anything but certain will surely suffer the consequences. Members of boards, as capable as they often are, can fall into this trap and end up rewarding the wrong behaviors.

The tension many of us feel when we are uncertain can be unbearable, causing us to jump to conclusions, what John Keats called "irritable reaching."[1] We seek an action that resolves the uncomfortable feeling of not knowing. Great leaders, however, resist the urge for quick but ill-advised solutions and skillfully push back on people who insist on answers to unanswerable questions.

Of course, we don't like doubt. Feeling sure of ourselves is far better, trusting we know what is true and that our decisions are correct. Generally people expect leaders to be sure of themselves and will excuse arrogance more than ambivalence. The feeling of uncertainty is so discomforting that we have little tolerance for it in others.

Most people avoid contradictory information, especially when it threatens their beliefs, and sometimes with the same vigor as if facing a physical threat. This can seem downright irrational, but it can be used as a clue. The idea that uncertainty and conflicting information should be avoided is a thinking trap, a cognitive error. And like all cognitive errors, it can be illuminated and mitigated by meta-cognition. It's a simple idea, but unfortunately it's sometimes difficult to act upon because discomfort gets in the way. When people are uncomfortable, the drive to rid themselves of pain can overtake even the most competent among us quite unwittingly. To resolve the tension, even if it is minor, people often take cognitive short-cuts. Unfortunately, these shortcuts, often used without awareness, may quash discomfort but raise the risk of bad decisions. The relief from removing tension is immediate, but the consequences of bad choices often show up later, even after the decision is long forgotten. To counteract this very human tendency, it is wise to adopt practices such as routinely studying failure followed by Charlie Munger.[2]

## Our Preference for Certainty

Researchers from Freud, who proposed that many psychiatric ailments are caused by a need to reduce anxiety, to psychologists and economists studying decision-making have illuminated the human preference for certainty. Three phenomena that are widely understood are overconfidence (the tendency to be too certain about our judgments and decisions), confirmation bias (the tendency to dismiss information that is inconsistent with what we believe), and binary bias (the tendency to lump information, experiences, and people into opposite categories like "smart" or "dumb," "beautiful" or "ordinary," and "educated" or "uneducated"). These are but three ways humans use shortcuts to reduce uncertainty, even though all lead to more mistakes.

These cognitive traps happen to everyone, and they are not a sign of weak intellect. They happen because of three things:

1 We are human. Our brains aren't computers, despite the metaphors we may use. Human cognition isn't perfectly accurate or reliably rational, but people can wrongly assume that their intention to be rational will guarantee it.

2 Confidence is a prized quality in people. Successful people are often described as confident, and leaders who appear so are more influential than those who are more circumspect.

3 Appearing uncertain may come at the cost of influence and career growth.

The tension between certainty and uncertainty originates within a person and is also affected by context. Yet, when people see what they perceive as uncertainty in a leader, they can worry. If the leader doesn't know, how can anyone trust that leader? This is a particular problem when an organization is facing a significant change or is in crisis. The temptation for leaders is to act sure, even when they are not, and to avoid saying the words, "I don't know." This tendency is aided and abetted by advisors who understand that a leader will be criticized if they appear to lack confidence and that people may assume the leader is headed for the exit—and they might be right.

I recall the oil spill in the Gulf of Mexico caused by an explosion on an oil rig owned by British Petroleum (BP). When Tony Hayward, then CEO of BP, finally appeared in public, he was in the throes of a crisis that included the loss of human lives and an environmental disaster. He was visibly and understandably upset and in the grip of great uncertainty. Beyond what was known, there was ambiguity on several fronts. What would be the extent of the damage? How would this event affect BP? What would it take to remediate the environmental damage? How would lives be altered? What infrastructure was damaged?

In situations such as the BP crisis, leaders need tremendous self-control so they do not succumb to false certainty or appear overwhelmed. If a leader hasn't been willing to say "I don't know" in less dire situations, they won't do so when the stakes are sky high. It was obvious that much was unknown, but Hayward faltered, saying, "I'd like my life back." At that point, I knew he was done, not because I knew him or thought he was a terrible person, but because he would be judged for his ill-considered remarks. The media, the public, his shareholders, and especially people in the Gulf region would surely insist that he be shown his way out. I can't blame those who judged him harshly, but I could see this was a man dealing with tremendous uncertainty as well as tragic loss.

The BP disaster is an example of how treacherous it can be to navigate the tension between certainty and uncertainty. Leaders usually prefer to be sure of themselves and their circumstances, but meta-leadership offers an option: Be certain of your ability to figure things out and confident that your colleagues will do the right things—*and* be willing to say what you know and don't know.

# We use shortcuts to reduce uncertainty and make decisions faster, but they also make us more prone to error.

During high-risk situations when deliberate, intentional thinking and inquiry are most needed, leaders may feel the greatest pressure to act confidently and do so reflexively. Yet, ironically, when the stakes are deemed low, the identical default thinking and actions likely occur because the mental work to make a deliberate decision doesn't seem worth the effort.

The trouble with determining the level of risk is complicated by the human need to be sure. James Lam, an expert on risk and director of RiskLens, describes three categories of risk: strategic, financial, and operational. His research, and others he cites, demonstrates the dichotomy of certainty and uncertainty. Lam asserts that some boards hold to processes and metrics that are easy to use but don't tell them what is really going on.[3] Too often, they settle for simple over accurate measures because they unwittingly equate simple with pragmatic and complicated with irrelevant.

For example, although strategic risk is the cause of the most significant losses, companies spend more time and money managing financial and operational risks. Why? Financial and operational risks are easier to control and measure. Strategic risk is more ambiguous, and boards tend to spend far less time asking questions in this area. Since boards usually comprise intelligent, experienced people who have successful track records, this is somewhat surprising—unless you consider that they are humans with the same tendency to be comforted by knowing more in the areas that are easier to examine.

## Between Uncertainty and Irrational Behavior

One critical decision leaders make is selecting people. For example, a board has the vital task of choosing the chief executive officer of a corporation, often described as their most important job. But any leader makes high-stakes decisions when they hire people. And yet often experienced people use "gut instinct" or simply move an employee from one role to another without assessing that person in light of different requirements. In such cases, we oversimplify but may do so with great confidence, even overlooking ourselves as the root of mistakes.

When we do recognize our own scant knowledge, we may take a different sort of shortcut by granting decision-making authority to someone we believe has more knowledge and experience, such as

- physicians, who possess breadth of knowledge of the human body;

- pharmacists, for deep knowledge of the effects of medications and especially in combination;

- financial managers, who make investment decisions on our behalf; and

- structural engineers, who specify how to build safe and strong buildings, bridges, and dams.

How do we decide who, within a particular specialty, to trust? We ask our friends and colleagues. We look for people whose knowledge and skill we trust instead of seeking the equivalent knowledge ourselves. This makes sense because learning enough about medicine, pharmacology, finance, or engineering to assess each person's capability is simply impossible. Leaders need expert advice, but it should not carry undue weight. Dr. Erika H. James, dean of the Wharton School of the University of Pennsylvania, and co-author Dr. Lynn Perry Wooten, president of Simmons University, write in *The Prepared Leader: Emerge from Any Crisis More Resilient Than Before* about the need for expert opinion: "To become a prepared leader, you should understand that empowering your team to lead is not the same as abdicating responsibility or delegating critical decision-making to others."[4] In a crisis, emotions run high and even top leaders can succumb to the appeal of relying on an expert when the stakes are high and time is short.

The world of fine art is, reputedly, chock full of fraud but also has many experts. It's easy to see why it is a breeding ground for dishonesty, but also mistakes. Even experts who know particular artists or genres exceptionally well can be fooled. When a scandal that destroyed the Knoedler Gallery was revealed, people immediately concluded that Ann Freedman, who ran the gallery for decades, was complicit in selling forgeries of abstract expressionist works supplied to the gallery by Glafira Rosales.[5] The documentary film that explores the situation, *Made You Look*, takes a deep dive into whether Freedman knew she was selling fake art.[6] In hindsight, the warning signs were there, but so were the reasons for her to think the works were legitimate. As more and more experts looked at the works alleged to be by artists such as Jackson Pollock, Mark Rothko, and Robert Motherwell, Freedman clung to confirmatory data, such as the opinions of experts who didn't realize they were giving an official judgment.

When people receive information that confirms what they already believe, it strengthens their beliefs. When presented with information or opinions that may cast doubt, all things being equal (and they never are), it seems logical that people would look carefully and perhaps reconsider their beliefs. Unfortunately, that isn't what happens most of the time.

When people look at fraud, with the benefit of hindsight and distance from the events, they tend to condemn people who are taken in, chirping a common refrain: "They should have known." But the investors in Bernie Madoff's notorious Ponzi scheme didn't think that the consistent returns on investments were cause for concern. Madoff had sterling referrals and happy clients—until everything unraveled.

Were there clues to the disasters looming at Enron, WorldCom, Tyco, and Countrywide? Of course. But from our armchair positions, we cannot see as effortlessly that there were also reasons to trust what was happening. To make decisions, we tend to employ the information most readily available to us, often from memory—what Daniel Kahneman and Amos Tversky call the availability heuristic.[7] So although it seems pretty logical to reach for data at hand, honestly critiquing such information once we have gathered and accepted it is more challenging.

## When "Better Results" Aren't Better

Richard Gilmore, senior vice-president and advisor at Raymond James, recalls a meeting he attended with executives of Wells Fargo. He asked an intelligent question, though he caught some criticism for it, about why the bank's retail business results were so much better than those of their peers. He was, quite rightly, noting that when something is better, it's a good idea to find out why. The results at Wells Fargo, touted by many, turned out to be so good because the company chased money at the expense of doing the right thing. Some of the activity was criminal, but all of it resulted from dreadful leadership and bad management decisions.

Recently, while listening to an earnings call, I noticed that after the CEO and CFO touted tremendous results, no one asked *how* these results were obtained. In one or two specific cases, the leaders spontaneously offered up explanations, all credible and highly conceptual. "Innovation" topped the list. They did an excellent job of building trust. So much so that the analysts accepted all the data reported without inquiry.

Of course, the dynamic at play in these calls also relates to the reputation of the analyst. By and large, analysts are well-informed people, and they come prepared with questions—or, perhaps I should say, they come distracted by their preparation. The questions are almost all predictable and rarely reflect the mental agility it takes to synthesize the information being delivered on the calls. If the analysts come to a call with certainty that their prepared questions are the right ones, it's tough for them to pivot to ask something else. There is time pressure and a boss back at the office who is interested in their performance. Asking a question the analyst is sure is good enough might be better than reacting to new information or even information that has been presented before and not questioned. After all, if it's such a good question, why didn't anyone ask it sooner?

## Position, Authority, and Fame Don't Convey Immunity

Most people recognize that leaders have significant influence; it is also true that social context influences leaders. It is far from a one-way street. This is an essential but often overlooked factor. For example, leaders often say they feel pressure to show others that they are sure of themselves. Even though many are aware of this demand, few recognize the force of it or realize the multiple channels through which it is exerted.

One way in which top executive officers are held to account is through legal mechanisms, such as the responsibility to truthfully report business results and make honest forecasts, known as "guidance." In addition, in the wake of major corporate scandals in the US, Congress enacted new legislation to protect investors, upping the ante for top leaders and putting prosecution of them, individually, on the table. Legal means create an obvious demand, as does the requirement to deliver financial results, but the less evident pressures are far more numerous, and many are not static. For example, people expect leaders to be aware of and sensitive to social justice and equity issues in and outside the workplace.

None of the leaders I work with denies the benefits of continuing to learn and grow, but they may be less confident in some areas than others. So how can a leader learn, which requires vulnerability, and still be confident? Asking the question this way reveals a dichotomy that suggests "learning" and "being certain" are opposite. Not true. People can begin to resolve this tension by shifting to a more nuanced look at certainty. Instead of certainty being based on what a person knows and can do, certainty can be based on the confidence they have in learning and integrating new information. Skill is seen not as a set of specific behaviors but as a capability, much like a springboard.

One of the most effective ways leaders can show the importance of learning is to do so themselves and in public. Although some leaders may feel unsure in such spontaneous circumstances and can easily say their schedules simply don't allow time, touring facilities and asking questions is a marvelous way to be public about their learning, as is asking employees at all levels questions about what they do, their aspirations, ideas, and background. Allowing a conversation to wander a bit isn't a waste of time; it shows interest and can be illuminating.

In this way, leaders can take a cue from scientists. Scientists use methods as much as they rely on facts and beliefs. A method requires that scientists change their minds and even the path of inquiry they have chosen in the face of new and better evidence. For example, in early 2020, when medical professionals realized they were dealing with a viral illness they hadn't seen before, clinicians did their best to help people who were ill with what we would later understand to be a novel virus. Meanwhile, researchers worked feverishly to learn about the pathogen and how it is transmitted. In the months that followed, scientists learned more, and sometimes new data forced new recommendations.

When we are scared, it can be challenging to remember that scientific inquiry is not a toggle switch. We can get frustrated and

"If someone is really certain about something, they have almost certainly frozen their ability to change their mind when they need to."

———

**CAROL TAVRIS**

mistrustful when public health officials say one thing at a point in time and another later. We want certainty, especially when we feel threatened. But the need to be sure must not over-ride the duty of scientists to use rigorous methods and skepticism until they have plenty of evidence. Great scientists can be certain and uncertain at the same time, and they can change what they think when the data tells them they must. However, this does not grant them immunity from criticism.

## Beyond the Idea of Heroic Leadership

Holding tight to our beliefs is a characteristic of human beings, and we're barely conscious of most of what we believe. What we know to be true is too vast to contemplate in our everyday lives. We need to take some things for granted to leave energy and room for higher-order thinking, such as strategy and the complexity of human relationships. However, the comfort and ease of taking what we know for granted is the very thing that can interfere with learning new things. Learning isn't always adding on, and sometimes it requires us to let go of what we believed yesterday. This is hard for humans, particularly because people tend to prize certainty and associate courage with "sticking to our guns." Sometimes to our detriment.

Often, we saddle leaders with the requirement to know and to be sure about what they know. A familiar and compelling, though not literal, image of a leader is of a person wearing a cape. Someone who knows the answers and is very confident. Someone who doesn't waver or act uncertain. Comforting though it may be, this image of leaders is unreasonable. Leaders aren't characters, even when they adopt a heroic persona that creates distance between themselves and others. People may come to see leaders as a caricature. Leaders themselves may feel saddled with their stereotypical notions of what a leader should be like. In both cases, heroes are vulnerable when they can't admit uncertainty, lack of knowledge, or mistakes. Maintaining the image is a breeding ground for dishonesty.

As success and a heroic image become reified and the accolades pile up, so too does the danger. A common but surprising cause of bad decisions is past success. Leaders who make excellent decisions in one situation may assume that the thought process they use, much like an immutable law, is transferrable. But failing to account for context can cause big decision mistakes. This tendency to overgeneralize is common and especially acute in the hero leader, or what some would call the "know-it-all." Early in my career as a consulting psychologist, my mentor, Dr. Joe McGill, said something I've never forgotten: "Never believe your own press." At first, I understood his comment to refer to our clients, all of whom were intelligent, successful executives. Later, I realized the maxim applied to me as well.

People needn't have an inflated ego to be vulnerable to the error of overgeneralizing; it happens to intelligent people who are honestly trying to do their best. Feeling a need for certainty is a clue that we may be reaching for a conclusion prematurely. A more powerful indication is vocal disdain for not knowing, whether we recognize it in ourselves or others.

Two things conspire to complicate our ability to see things as they are. The first is feeling sure of oneself. Confidence is an admired and helpful attribute in leaders, but too much can make others feel obliged to bend to a leader's ideas even when they are ill advised. The second is the social and interpersonal context. While most people recognize the significant influence of leaders, we often overlook the effect of context. Leaders often feel pressure to show others they are confident; even arrogance might be tolerated if the results are good.

With that in mind, how can we use confidence as well as be alert to how it may create risk?

## "How Am I Thinking?"

So much of our discourse is about *what* to do and *how* to do it. Leaders are often praised for being action oriented and confident. All of these factors conspire to create habits that save time but also create the risk that we will act reflexively when a more thoughtful approach is required. Tuning in to how we think and under what circumstances can lead to priceless insight that helps us reduce risks that come from oversimplification. The alternative is to be at the mercy of habit and convenient, but not necessarily great, role models.

Habits have the advantage of imbuing us with a sense of competence and can be useful in routine tasks where risks are low but over-ride our ability to detect faint signals that risk levels are changing and need our attention. Routinized strategic planning processes, for example, may be technically rigorous but myopic. Kodak is an example, as are Blockbuster and BlackBerry, each at one time a powerhouse; but each failed to see looming threats until it was too late.

Fortunately, there are people who use a meta-approach to help them stay attuned to how they are thinking, as well as what. Two who spring to mind are Jim Cramer and Carol Tavris.

Jim Cramer is the host of *Mad Money* and co-anchor of the 9 a.m. hour of *Squawk on the Street*, both on CNBC. Cramer is provocative and expresses his pointed opinions with great certainty and high volume. He's not everyone's cup of tea, but he is an example of the value of thinking about thinking. First, he admits mistakes. He openly says, when he believes it warranted, "I was wrong." These admissions don't end his career; far from it, they make him more credible. He admits error, and then he explains what led him to it. This is as valuable as the admission! Second, my favorite of his sayings is "buy and homework," modifying the adage that one should buy and hold investments. Why is this important? Because it acknowledges that circumstances change, markets shift, and leaders come and go.

Dr. Carol Tavris, a social psychologist, approaches the process of decision-making from the perspective of a scientist. She is noted for her contributions to rational thinking, debunking myths, and correcting mistakes, even those celebrated in peer-reviewed research. Tavris's devotion to the truth makes her willing to admit her own mistakes and point out errors made by others. One reason she chose social psychology (rather than comparative literature) as her career was that she "liked the idea of testing ideas for their relative validity," and she liked that her research had immediate beneficial applications for people's private lives, relationships, and society.[8] Tavris speaks openly about her commitment to rigorous research and avoiding what she terms "hysteria," sometimes seen in public opinion. She has publicly stated that she was mistaken in her views of a scandal that swept the US over allegations that a daycare center was systematically abusing children. She could have "stood her ground," but instead, she found the ground she was standing on wasn't solid. She changed her mind, admitted error, and used this experience to teach.

Leaders who are willing to change their minds in the face of more, better, or new information accept the risk that they will be criticized for being wishy-washy or lacking confidence. However, in these cases, leaders can be teachers and role models, helping others understand that while certainty about principles and values is important, so is allowing uncertainty to fuel curiosity.

## DECIDING WITH INSIGHT

The next time you face a decision, big or small, pause and ask yourself if the certainty-uncertainty dichotomy is affecting your thinking and judgment:

1   Does my position, reputation, or relationships demand I make a particular decision?

2   What is my level of discomfort with not knowing in this situation?

3   If I make a terrible decision, am I willing to take responsibility? If so, will I engage others in postmortem analysis for the sake of learning?

# 2

# The Most Rational among Us Can Be Irrational

We love to praise rationality and dismiss ideas
that seem outlandish as irrational.
But without fantastic ideas, there is no
innovation, only incremental improvements
until we realize no one cares.

THE DIMENSIONS of rationality and irrationality can assume mythical proportions. Indeed, they are dramatized in archetypes from Greek mythology. The story goes that Zeus had two sons: Apollo, the sun god, and Dionysus, the god of wine and dance. Apollo symbolizes logic, purity, and rational thinking, while Dionysus represents chaos, emotion, and instincts. The beauty of myths is that they metaphorically crystalize essential aspects of human beings, embodying abstract concepts in vivid form.

The tension expressed by the myth of Apollo and Dionysus is readily seen in modern life, and we often prefer one or the other. "Apollonian" refers to people who rely on numbers, facts, and hard data. In contrast, others value a more "Dionysian" approach using intuition, feelings, and qualitative information. Exploring the archetypes of Apollo and Dionysus can show what it costs us when we value one way of thinking to the exclusion of all others.

What do we do when considering the symbols of Apollo and Dionysus?

- See them as entertainment. Enjoy, then forget them.

- Think about people we know who have Apollonian or Dionysian characteristics.

- Use some new language to describe ourselves and others, a new label.

What is harder to do, and rarer, is to ask, "What aspects of *each* character do I see in others and myself?" and, "What can I learn from this?"

When leaders place extreme value on logic and quantitative data, it inclines them to rationalize away other information types. Sometimes leaders are overt in their disdain for qualitative data, labeling it irrational and silencing those who might add valuable information. Conversely, when leaders prefer experiential or observational data, they may be critical of quantitative data and statistical analysis, overlooking what these may reveal. One or the other type of information doesn't tell us everything we might need, or want, to know.

## Stumbling On Success

John, an executive vice-president, and his human resources colleague Helen interviewed Barbara, a candidate for senior vice-president. John and Helen planned to offer Barbara the job at a dinner, but when she showed up fifteen minutes late wearing ripped jeans and a T-shirt, and then repeatedly interrupted the server, they held back. The next day, they jointly decided that despite her egregious behavior, it was unfair to Barbara to use subjective impressions and their personal opinions to withhold the offer.

Immediately after joining the company, Barbara proved that they should not have ignored their observations or their discomfort with what they saw. John and Helen not only ignored their reactions; they dismissed the significance of Barbara's behavior. For the two of them, being illogical and not foregrounding quantitative data for a decision was tantamount to stupidity. To hide their fears of looking foolish, they relied on language of the company culture, which emphasized rationality, logic, and data-driven decisions, without realizing they had more relevant data. Sadly, many in the company were in the habit of ignoring behavioral data and over-relying on questionable paper-and-pencil tests, most of them invalid. Even more regrettable, their company stubbornly clung to their hiring process despite many bad decisions that cost them financially, dinged their reputation, and slowed progress.

Ironically, one division of this company did a great job of hiring, and they were equally committed to a data-driven approach. The difference was that the team that made good decisions promoted most people into executive roles from inside the organization. They had tons of performance data on candidates but also tremendous knowledge of their reputations. Unfortunately, they stumbled on success without realizing they were using both hard facts *and* social proof, which is opinion based.

The leaders of this company were all smart and experienced, but they were using partial information as a proxy for the whole person. We often do this, especially when something is as complex as understanding people.

We can use behavioral data by doing the following:

- **Focus on observable behavior.** Observable behavior is what someone does or says rather than the meaning we ascribe to it. For example, Barbara was often late to meetings. That is behavior. What the behavior means is less important than its effect on others.

- **Define how behaviors are relevant to the job.** Barbara was expected to be on time to meetings because it is the company norm, it sets a good example for others, and it shows respect. All are relevant to her role.

- **Observe whether the behavior is repeated.** Behaviors that recur are more telling than one-time events. Reacting strongly to an anomalous behavior isn't usually wise. The exceptions to this "rule" are egregious violations of trust, malfeasance, or inappropriate interpersonal behavior, all of which deserve swift and strong reaction.

- **Identify if the behaviors are individual, group, or widespread.**
  Disregarding the context causes leaders to ascribe blame to
  individuals when, sometimes, problems are caused by a destructive culture, bad management, weak systems, or inadequate
  resources.

Barbara had been in her role scarcely sixty days when the com-
plaints began rolling in. The criticisms were delivered, as we might
expect, in the language of the corporate culture. She wasn't "but-
toned up," her plans were too "loose," and she often changed her
mind. It was causing great consternation among her colleagues.

By the time the company asked for my help, Barbara was already
in trouble, but she didn't understand why. She said her colleagues
didn't give her enough latitude to learn the ropes, and she was angry
and hurt. Her boss was concerned about her but also about himself, since her failure would mean egg on his face. After spending
time with John, Helen, and Barbara's team members, I realized what
had probably happened. During the selection process, Barbara had
shown only small clues that she was a poor fit for the role, until the
fateful dinner, when she arrived late in unprofessional attire and was
rude to the server.

Barbara's colleagues provided more information of the same
type—she was chronically late and constantly interrupted people.
In less than fourteen months, John fired her due to abysmal performance and for alienating most of her colleagues. But he agonized
so long before removing Barbara that his reputation was tarnished.
However, he was willing to look back on the events. Although he was
undoubtedly culpable in a wrong decision and was indecisive once
he realized it, the organization's culture played a role. The emphasis
on complex data, frequent and overt criticism of observational data,
and repetitive use of language that steered leaders to spreadsheets
more than conversation were very influential.

"There is only one thing that makes a dream impossible to achieve: the fear of failure."

---

**PAULO COELHO**

## In Praise of Delusion

In our culture, "delusion" is almost always used to describe a weak grasp of reality or perhaps a severe mental illness. But there is a different way to think about fantasies: as fuel for creativity and innovation.

Leaders talk a lot about innovation but too often fear the things associated with building a culture that supports game-changing ideas. Leaders want big ideas but nothing too wild; they want to create the next revolution, not be subject to it, but they may also find it hard to tolerate views that start out sounding like science fiction. Successful, game-changing ideas can appear fantastical or even delusional, but making it normal to let these ideas see the light of day is what successful innovators do.

On a memorable trip with a colleague with whom I frequently travelled, I said in exasperation, "Come and talk to me when I can have my phone, calendar, and email in a device the size of my cell phone." We were sitting on a plane, headed back from Mexico City, tired from work and loaded down with pottery we'd bought at a local market. It seemed that juggling was our profession. We had crowded schedules, were on planes constantly, navigated places we'd never been, and kept track of our clients' advice about how not to get kidnapped. (I'm not joking.) We needed to access maps, hotel information, schedules, plane reservations, the client's name and title, and often how to pronounce it properly. We had lots of paper, computers, and cell phones, but nothing like what is available now. Little did I know that I would have such a device within two years and that now the same device allows me to do a zillion other practical, fun, and helpful things.

I also have vivid memories of standing in the yard of my childhood home in Cocoa Beach, Florida, watching unmanned launches from Cape Canaveral and the space center that had not yet been named for President Kennedy. The rockets, which did not have astronauts aboard at that time, would routinely explode. When the explosions happened at night, it was a spectacular light show that was beautiful and scary.

Many of the grown-ups in town worked in the space program or had jobs related to it—as engineers, physicists, mathematicians, computer programmers, test pilots, project managers, and so on— and most were men. These were the dads who often built things in their garages, knew how to fix cars, and tended to be a little distant. Nevertheless, they were the epitome of rationality to my child's mind. I believed they would figure out how to get people into space but also realized I had no idea how they would do it. The people who worked to get humans into space and on the moon eventually made what had appeared irrational real.

When science fiction writer Arthur C. Clarke talked about the future and how people would use computers, it certainly didn't seem rational. In a 1964 episode of the BBC science documentary show *Horizon*, Clarke portended a time when people would be able to work from anywhere in the world because computers would connect us. It sounded outlandish when he said it in 1964, but here we are.

What allows some people to hold on to what may seem irrational and allow science, technology, and engineering to catch up? A few qualities:

- Tolerance for ideas that have no obvious way to come to life yet
- Resistance to ridicule
- Understanding that human beings want to explore, literally and in our minds
- The ability to withstand popular ideas in favor of enduring truths

And what of more routine matters, like running a business that needs to constantly create, or one that is technical and scientific but needs to attract and retain people who are technically skilled and can manage other humans? The most talented people don't always want to lead other gifted people. The messiness of people can be a deterrent to leaders learning how to be good managers and lead well. An engineering company that wants to grow revenue and margin and enter new markets can't do it with technical skill alone. And businesses that need artists, like Pixar, have the same problem even though it appears the opposite. As much as an engineer might not want to be involved in things that require too much interpersonal effort, an artist could have equal dislike for business-related matters such as budgets.

The issue is that a person's professional identity can inhibit their thinking and decision-making by relying on stereotypical dichotomies: either a person is rational, as an engineer or scientist is, or they are irrational, like an artist. Don't we all know artists who struggle to earn money? Indeed, we've all met someone highly technical and data-driven who will analyze the cost per mile of a trip that is supposed to be fun, perhaps driving other people up the wall in the process.

People who have the ability to create do so in their minds first. Some notable examples:

- Ted Turner, who launched CNN without a background in broadcasting

- Jeff Bezos, who started selling books online and was dismissed as a kooky guy with an outlandish laugh

- Elon Musk, who remains a popular object of jabs, but who keeps creating what he first imagines

- Arthur C. Clarke, who dared to predict that someday humans would be instantly connected to each other by computers

- The "Imagineers" at Disney, who invent new technologies to be used for entertainment

Walt Disney's Imagineers were so aptly named because the term merges two essential qualities for innovation: imagination and a way to make it come to life. This corresponds perfectly with rationality and irrationality. Imagination allows us to push aside the limitations of what we know or think we know. Holding on to what we imagine, even though it *does not yet exist*, instead of dismissing it, allows our brains time to figure things out. Engineering, literal or metaphorical, is a method for the hard work of figuring things out by testing, failing, and trying again until something works, or until we give up.

## Dangerous Delusions

When a scandal erupts, people are quick to blame. Often the finger-pointing comes with judgments about the central figure(s)' lack of ethics, character, morals, or all of the above. This is well deserved when someone orchestrates fraud, but sometimes what looks like a fraud is more complex. Dangerous delusions that are not caused by mental illness can happen even to brilliant people.

When health technology company Theranos was started and sought investment, the company and its founder, Elizabeth Holmes, attracted well-known and respected people. Henry Kissinger, George Shultz, and William Foege (former director of the Centers for Disease Control and Prevention) were board members. Investors included Rupert Murdoch and several large venture capital and private equity firms. The company was developing blood tests using small amounts of blood rather than the multiple tubes often required for routine tests. Holmes said that her drive to establish a new technology was based on her love for an uncle. She said he had an illness for which the treatment meant frequent blood tests, which added to his suffering. The story is compelling, as is the idea that a machine could do a comprehensive analysis of blood with a tiny sample from a finger stick, rather than a vein puncture.

Holmes was credible, and as more investors joined, she and the company began racking up what is known as social proof. This concept is essential in understanding how people gain influence through association with respectable people. The term was coined by Robert Cialdini, an expert on influence who has researched the phenomenon for decades. When people face something uncertain, they often look to others for indications about what to do or not to do.[1] We copy others, though we are often reluctant to recognize the power of the social environment, claiming our decisions are independent. The power of social proof also reassures us if we question a decision but others are sticking to theirs.

Once Murdoch was involved in Theranos, it became a more credible enterprise. But the story of Theranos is one of deceit. Holmes and her business partner, Ramesh Balwani, never demonstrated the technology for which they received hundreds of millions of dollars in investment. Ultimately, the two were charged with fraud, and, at the time of writing, the cases are still making their way through the courts. This shows that even knowledgeable and experienced people can, quite unwittingly, rely on evidence that isn't credible. Further, it can be so difficult to admit error or contemplate significant loss that people will "double down," defending a decision when they should question it. The danger to investors in Theranos was financial loss and perhaps reputational damage. But the losses were potentially far more consequential to patients whose medical providers relied on test results that were not valid.

I mentioned *Made You Look* in the previous chapter. This documentary about fake art depicts a classic story of deception made possible by cognitive biases run amok. Ann Freedman, the director of the Knoedler Gallery in New York City, was apparently fooled into purchasing sixty forgeries that the gallery resold for $80 million. It is the most significant scandal involving art forgery in American history. In the documentary, art experts, attorneys, journalists, and people who paid millions for a single painting weigh in on Freedman's intentions, what she knew or should have known. Most judge her harshly, especially for believing the credibility of an obscure dealer who had access to so many undiscovered works by acclaimed artists, including Jackson Pollock and Mark Rothko.

How does a successful, knowledgeable person like Freedman fall for such a scam? Not without help—lured as she was by a deceptive seller, encouraged by sophisticated buyers, and vulnerable to the needs of the Knoedler Gallery for revenue. This is an explosive combination and, eventually, it was discovered, but not until more than $80 million in fake paintings were sold.

The art fooled collectors and experts, but not everyone. Scrutiny by some led to suspicions. However, acknowledging outright that a painting is fake, even when an expert says so, can cause a legal fight that is embarrassing, costly, and emotionally exhausting. As a result, even renowned experts may be reluctant to make stark declarations in favor of opinions that cast doubt, but stop short of declaring a work fraudulent.

## Skeptical, Not Cynical

Leaders promoting a significant investment often seek dissenting views about the wisdom of their ideas, right? Well, maybe. Warren Buffett and Charlie Munger are well known for their deliberate decisions, and their track record is a testament to the value of their process. They aim to buy shares in companies of good quality that are undervalued. The strategy has led to less volatility while still taking prudent risks. This has paid off for those seeking good returns without a roller-coaster ride that some investors simply don't have the stomach to withstand.

Buffett and Munger are appropriately skeptical, asking questions about why something is such a good deal or how a company explains its superior performance compared to its industry peers. These are

# The brilliant future we imagine is unattainable if we insist on guarantees of perfection.

———

essential questions but yield far better information if the answers aren't merely conceptual jargon. For example, "We simply deliver better customer service," is neither a complete nor rational answer. Tell us what "better" looks like. Is that real, or are your employees simply pressuring people? This was the story behind the mess at Wells Fargo, which senior leaders said they knew nothing about.

The truth about what was happening at Wells Fargo is that front-line employees were given unreasonable goals for opening new accounts and were pressured to meet the goals. The intensity was so great that they began convincing customers to open accounts they didn't need or want. In some cases, employees falsified information to meet unreasonable quotas and escape the threat of losing their jobs. While those who met the quotas kept their jobs, many paid a different price: they suffered emotionally because they felt ashamed.

Ultimately, Wells Fargo paid $3 billion to settle an investigation by the Department of Justice and the Securities and Exchange Commission.[2] The chief executive, John G. Stumpf, was fired and agreed to pay a $17.5 million fine.

Investors who are rational, even a "buy and hold" investor like Berkshire Hathaway, aren't immune to mistakes. They know that their evaluation of a company for investment, no matter how rationally a person does this, is pinned to a point in time. Things change, and investors need to keep watching. Recall Jim Cramer's phrase, "buy and homework" (instead of "buy and hold"). His approach acknowledges that a decision to invest may be rational and reasonable at one point in time, but it is irrational to hold on to an investment solely because it was once great.

Cramer, Buffett, and Munger have something in common: they admit mistakes. Berkshire Hathaway's annual reports tell investors what mistakes they made and what it cost. But, unlike art dealer Ann Freedman, they don't wait until they have no choice but to admit error; they do so quickly. Investors in Theranos held on, defending the company and Holmes, when they would have been better off making more inquiries. Curiously, sometimes we take great care to investigate an opportunity before committing, then cling to our decision even after seeing signs that it wasn't in our best interest. The dynamic happens in investments in financial assets, real estate, friendships, and business and personal partnerships.

Loss aversion exerts a powerful influence on our thinking and decisions. Often described as the tendency for people to avoid financial loss, it applies to other kinds of loss as well. For example, losses involving relationships, reputation, and status are also powerful motivators, if not always apparent.

## Moving from Knowledge to Wisdom

How can people make better use of both rational *and* irrational thinking? Is it possible? It is, and we can learn to incorporate both qualities of thinking more often.

How do we incorporate rational and irrational thinking without going too far one way or another? First, meta-cognition, which, as a reminder, simply means thinking about thinking, is helpful because it focuses on *what* we believe, think, and decide, and *how*. Second, we can admit and look for the benefits of what we believe is rational and what we feel is irrational. Third, we can acknowledge that there are differences in how we and others think and decide, and that we also make rapid and sometimes rigid judgments that make us feel secure and keep us stuck.

To accomplish this introspective task, we can ask ourselves some questions. When answered honestly, they can reveal a great deal. Making what is outside our awareness conscious is a lever we can use for more deliberate decisions. But, of course, we can always choose to be spontaneous when the stakes are low.

Anyone honest will admit that they sometimes wonder, "What was I thinking?" I guess that we all have looked back on choices made decades ago and realized, even out loud, that we made a dumb decision—usually about something of little consequence. Of course, distance in time makes it easier, but how do we examine a decision we are contemplating? A significant investment, for example?

- **What are the tangible and intangible gains?** Framing the question this way opens us up to recognize both obvious and subtle gains influencing us.

- **Who am I attempting to please? Who do I want to avoid annoying or disappointing?** Even in boardrooms, there are concerns about people's feelings, and these can wield a surprising influence on decisions. A board of directors may yield to a retiring CEO, for example, purely to avoid upsetting them, and perhaps ignoring the effect on talented people in the company who are eager and capable of taking on more responsibility.

- **What pressures am I experiencing to make one decision or another?** People don't exist in a vacuum; social context is real and powerful. This is why culture, whether of a small group or large multinational organization, matters.

- **Are there opinions that I minimize and dismiss because I don't like them?** I have observed a pattern that is quite robust when people hear my assessment of a situation and they don't like what I have to say. But, of course, it happens when the evaluation is unflattering. First, they disagree. Second, they criticize my method. Third, they attack me personally.

In *Made You Look*, we see Ann Freedman demonstrate this pattern. Upon learning the results of an expert analysis of a particular painting that had come under great scrutiny, Freedman disagreed with the assessment and criticized the method and the expert. But, intentional or not, she missed the opportunity to stop herself from continuing down a path that would lead to scandal. Freedman later admitted that she had been fooled, but not until it was undeniable.

The opinions about Freedman's involvement in the fraud vary widely. Some say she knew; others say she should have known. Both are easy to say about a person and circumstance from a distance. It's harder to appreciate how much influence context has on our thinking and decisions. We're more likely to see people like Freedman as flawed individuals who behaved irrationally.

However, for years, Freedman successfully ran the gallery and perpetuated its good reputation. She had to use both love for art and business acumen and seems to have done so. The Dionysian intuition and emotion about beautiful works of art seems to be part of Freedman's makeup, and she freely spoke about "falling in love" with art. The buyers were equally swept away, with one saying, "I have the opportunity to buy a Rothko?" and being clearly moved by the sight of a work of art (this one wasn't authentic, but that wasn't obvious).

But an Apollonian aspect had also played a role in Freedman's decisions. She had to buy art that she knew could be sold at a healthy profit and needed not just paintings but also provenance attached to the works. Provenance refers to the origin, the record of who owned the art after the artist and the chain of ownership to the present. Freedman was no stranger to the need for provenance, but at the time she began to acquire the forgeries, she allowed her desire to acquire them to over-ride her more logical thinking.

Sometimes, the Dionysian impulse has too much sway and leads even smart people to make decisions that appear foolish to others, but it can be exhilarating. The Apollonian aspect can be a dullard, a cynic, and a killjoy that is extremely annoying.

Leaders who achieve great things are neither completely rational nor always irrational, nor do they subscribe to rigid methods to make sure they don't go off the deep end in either direction. Instead, they have the ability to step back and examine *how* they are thinking and what is influencing them. This is the cognitive aspect of meta-leadership.

## SHARPEN THE FOCUS ON OBSERVABLE BEHAVIOR

Pair observations of a behavior with its effect:

1   Think about what it might mean when someone is chronically late. How many descriptions can you come up with? *Notice how easy it is to do this.*

2   Imagine you need to give feedback to the person who is chronically late. *What would you say? What have you heard others say in a similar situation?*

3   Recall your own reaction when someone gives you negative feedback and interprets what your behavior means. *What is your reaction?*

4   Think about times when you have received positive feedback that includes attributions about your character or talent. *As good as it might feel, does it help you understand what you do particularly well, so you can repeat the behavior?*

3

# Strategy and Tactics Move the Needle

Archimedes said, "Give me a place to stand and with a lever I will move the world." His words encapsulate the value of strategy and tactics. Good leaders reach for the right lever based on what they are trying to do. Meta-leaders think first, then reach for the right lever because they know the most valuable tool is their mind.

CHERYL BACHELDER became CEO of Popeyes Chicken and Biscuits in 2007 when the company was struggling. Revenue was down, and franchisees were unhappy with and distrustful of "corporate." Bachelder says that sometimes the feeling was mutual. Fast food restaurants like Popeyes need clear procedures and a high level of standardization to ensure food safety and consistency. But adhering to tight processes without knowing where you are headed or why can become soul-sucking, routine. Eventually employees lose interest, and that leads to unhappy customers.

When Bachelder took the helm, the situation was bleak. But following a rebrand of the company as Popeyes Louisiana Kitchen, the chain racked up ten years of growth in a row. The stock price rose from $15 to $79, and franchisees saw dramatically improved sales and profits. Bachelder was an invited speaker at the Executive Women of Goizueta conference in Atlanta in 2019, followed by a fireside chat with me. She held us spellbound as she described her tenure at Popeyes.

Before Bachelder spoke, she showed a video of an orchestra and an interview with the conductor who spoke about his role of guiding, leading, inspiring, and unleashing the talents of each member of the orchestra. The analogy was obvious, but the music and sincerity of the conductor made it emotional. Bachelder spoke about leaders as conductors and the importance of serving those whom you lead. She spoke of vision and the importance of having a daring destination, what I refer to as strategic direction. Next, she shared the strategic priorities, listed on a single, uncluttered page, that had guided Popeyes through the turnaround:

1  Build a distinctive brand—invite the guest
2  Run great restaurants—delight the guest
3  Grow restaurant profits—make money
4  Accelerate quality restaurants—expand our footprint

Before this list came to be, the leadership team had been working on a list of 128 active projects but weren't getting them done. This is a common trap that even intelligent people fall into: using activity as a proxy for results. It gives tactics such a bad name that some leaders stand back from them in the belief that their work is strategic and shouldn't be concerned with tactics, as though engaging with them would somehow soil their hands.

There is truth to the idea that leaders needn't be in the weeds, but neither can they abide tactics that are disconnected from strategic direction. If the strategy isn't clear, then every tactic can be defended and perpetuated. When strategy is clear but the wrong tactics are employed, it is just like making great time heading in the wrong direction. These statements seem obvious, but it can be surprisingly difficult to see mismatches of strategy and tactics—unless leaders are standing in the right place.

## Thinking about Strategic Thinking

When a strategy fails, the blame often goes to poorly chosen or inadequately executed tactics. The phrase "We had a sound strategy, but our execution wasn't sufficient" gets leaders off the hook, much in the way that blaming culture clashes is an accepted excuse for acquisition or merger failures. Roger Martin, former dean of the Rotman School of Management at the University of Toronto, asks, in what field, other than business, do people proclaim that a strategy was brilliant when it failed? If a leader claims their strategy was brilliant, but it failed, they are dividing strategy and tactics. A CEO can't get off the hook by saying the direction of the company was sound but the people in the organization failed—or can they?

Martin's work conveys how much power a popular idea can have, even if it is completely wrong. He is renowned for his work on strategy, and his *Harvard Business Review* article "The Big Lie of Strategic Planning" lays out the traps that await leaders when thinking about strategy.[1] The traps are strategic planning, cost-based thinking, and self-referential frameworks. All three are traps because strategy is about setting a direction and making choices; it is hard and involves uncertainty and risk. Strategic planning gives people a sense of control and, because people don't like risk, especially when they may suffer personal losses as a result of their decisions, planning tends to overtake strategy creation.

Martin's advice is threefold, and excellent:

- **Keep it simple.** Capture your strategy in a one-pager that addresses where you will play and how you will win.

- **Don't look for perfection.** Strategy isn't about finding answers. It's about placing bets and shortening odds.

- **Make the logic explicit.** Be clear about what must change for you to achieve your strategic goal.

However, he and I part company when he says, "Reconcile yourself to feeling uncomfortable." My advice is, don't reconcile. Wrestle with discomfort using brains, emotion, and action. Engage completely, face the ambiguity, de-fog the mirror, make choices, and do not settle for mechanized strategy sessions.

It may sound comical, but there is profound truth in what Rita McGrath, professor at the Columbia Business School, says about strategic planning: "Most strategic planning exercises are budgeting in a Halloween costume!"[2] Why would McGrath be moved to make such a statement? Perhaps she's seen smart people work hard, believing they are creating strategy when, in fact, they are justifying budgets. It's backward, but not uncommon. Senior executives, seeking more money, people, space, maybe a bigger microphone, need to show that what they want is aligned with the strategy. People can be extremely creative in rationalizing, even believing their own story and defending it to their detriment.

The job of board members is to challenge strategic plans, yet too often, and perhaps attempting to avoid meddling, they err on the side of accepting them and the budgets that go alongside. Yes, they may ask about financial risks or capability—those are easier to assess than strategic risk—but not the source of the greatest risk.[3]

How is it that a group of intelligent, successful people can settle for so little from management? Three reasons:

1 Directors are human beings.
2 Strategy is hard.
3 Methodology and analysis are easier.

We can't change the first reason, but the others are subject to intellect and judgment for those who are willing to do the hard, often ambiguous work.

## Strategy is hard

It takes hard work to create a robust yet simple strategy. It's easier to analyze, look backward, and compare with prior results. Self-referential benchmarking is common because it's easy.

However, strategic exercises can create a sense of satisfaction so strong that it blots out the recognition that the output is a budget-based operating plan devoid of strategic choices. If board directors and senior executives are to choose wisely, they need to do

**Leaders needn't be in the weeds— but they can't abide tactics that are disconnected from strategic direction.**

———————

more than review; they need to think, think about their thinking, and consider what is influencing them. This simple change in approach opens up the mind to see beyond default decisions.

### Methodology is the easy way out

Legions of consultants have methods for strategy development. Most methods yield huge presentations that look great and contain a lot of analysis. The analyses are sometimes jokingly referred to as "rationalization," but they're no joke.

The essence of the strategy usually appears on the first page. Great leaders can articulate the strategy in clear language, as Bachelder did, while less capable leaders hide behind charts. Indeed, prior-year budgets and pro forma updates often have outsized influence over strategy processes. This is one reason why strategic planning processes often kill innovation. When there is no framework for risk assessment, the idea of investing is often too scary. Utter the word "risk," and some people become very unsettled, even if the risk has yet to be defined or studied. People can mistakenly lean toward "safe decisions" that aren't safe at all, just as keeping money in cash isn't risk free.

Most boards and senior executives routinely engage in strategic planning exercises. What's wrong with that? Maybe nothing. If your organization is performing well against objective measures of what matters most, then congratulations to you. If you understand *how* and *why* performance is good, even better. Finally, suppose you have a clear, simple, teachable framework for success that doesn't depend upon a heroic chief executive. In that case, you are on your way to guiding an organization that can achieve success over time.

## Strategy from a Meta-Perspective

Instead of being stuck in the dichotomy of choosing primarily to value either strategic thinking or tactical execution, and rather than handing strategy work off to consultants, leaders can improve their strategic thinking and strategy development. The following steps are a path to create strategy that fuels an organization:

**Be clear about what strategy is and isn't.** Strategy is about *what* we intend to become, not *how* we will get there. Strategic planning can drain the life out of strategic thinking. This is especially true when focusing on *how*, *when*, and *who*, giving little attention to *what* and *why*.

**Familiarize yourself with how you and your colleagues behave when you are uncomfortable.** Human beings don't like discomfort and prefer to avoid or reduce it in an endless number of ways. Courageous leaders can work through tensions while being honest with themselves and each other. A vibrant, courageous team can self-monitor and self-regulate. The best leaders are brave enough to routinely invite expert input and advice about how their teams function, including the strengths they leverage, as well as their collective habits and behaviors that interfere with them doing their best work.

**Call out default positions or decisions.** Leaders who frame conversations with the correct language can help an entire team slow down long enough to shift gears. Saying, "This is going to be tough," for example, can signal everyone to dial in not only to the content but to their own very understandable tendencies to take shortcuts when circumstances are hard.

**Be on the lookout for what distracts you.** Strategic conversations that turn to the tactical can be a way to avoid the complex and sometimes messy—but necessary—strategic dialog. Likewise, a bully can derail meaningful conversations by saying things like, "This is a waste of time; we all know what the answer is," or other bombastic, demeaning comments. A method to help groups avoid the well-known distractors is to take a few minutes, in advance of conversations, to name the barriers. What has distracted us in the past? What should we do differently this time? A short amount of time spent pre-thinking can keep the process out of the ditch.

**Engage leaders who must implement a strategy.** Senior executives and directors should know each other, and not just from formal presentations. If board members are too reliant on the opinion of the CEO about who can do what, they can't give their best advice. Likewise, when senior executives are too isolated from the board, they are vulnerable to what they don't know.

**Expect a one-page statement of strategic intent with no more than five priorities.** A strategy that can't be easily explained is almost certainly not strategic. The strategy should have a few key priorities and identified measures of success. It's not enough to say, "We'll be the greatest."

**Tie budget approval to the priorities.** If something shows up in a budget proposal that isn't related to the strategy, the discussion should come to a screeching halt. What is it? Why? There might be a great reason, but it could also be a way to keep one foot on the dock while trying to launch the boat—a plan that almost surely ends up with losses.

Imagine Archimedes, the Greek mathematician quoted at the opening of this chapter, claiming he was standing in the correct place, but that someone had handed him the wrong lever and, rather than moving the boulder, the lever broke. He is the creator of this idea and powerful image, grounded in mathematics, but he accepted a lever that someone else decided was adequate? I doubt it. The great mathematician would have specified what lever was needed or retrieved it himself.

Even intelligent leaders sometimes settle for weak levers that will break under pressure, especially when they aren't thinking about their own thinking and how they decide which tools are the right ones.

## Stereotypes Keep Us Stuck

Watch someone look through a kaleidoscope and ask them to describe what they see. It's fun and informative to discover how different people perceive and make sense of an entirely ambiguous image. Now ask them to turn the device and describe what they look at first and second. Finally, ask them to adjust the kaleidoscope again and look at the image any way they wish. Most people enjoy moving the kaleidoscope and often spontaneously describe the images. They might even recognize the parallels between a kaleidoscopic image and their family, community, company, or even the world.

A kaleidoscope shows us that small changes can produce large effects because it does more than change how the pieces are arranged; it changes the relationship of the pieces to one another. It also might suggest that we don't see or understand the pieces themselves until they can be observed in different circumstances—a lot like people. Of course, the turquoise glass in a kaleidoscope will never be orange or red, but it will play a different role within the whole design, depending on all the other pieces.

Sometimes, leaders have a hard time stepping away from a method they rely on, especially if they have had success with it— almost as if they developed a design that was pleasing, and so they can't bring themselves to turn the dial on their lens, even if the circumstances have changed.

If someone swiped your kaleidoscope and replaced some pieces, when you moved the device, it would produce distinctly different results. But that is fun and games, and what sort of a bore wouldn't play with a cool device like that for a couple minutes? Yet, when the stakes are even higher, the drive to explore, even in our own minds or in conversation, often gives way to fear, and this, in turn, can cause us to lean on stereotypes. Relying on the familiar and predictable makes things simpler, but at a cost.

Resorting to stereotypes might be a wise tactic of choice, but some can't seem to step away from them when doing so would be best—when the circumstances change, for example. People naturally develop patterns of behavior based on what has worked well, or on what hasn't worked well, in the past. When these patterns also fit a stereotype, such as "accountants love detail" or "designers are creative but impractical," people find it hard to break free. This isn't only because of how we see ourselves but also because of how others see us—as one thing or another, and utterly unchangeable.

At one time, my professional growth was limited by how I saw myself based, in part, on feedback I received from teachers. They despaired of me never "living up to my potential" because I wasn't a good student, even though I performed exceptionally well on standardized tests. Years later, I realized that my thinking is naturally conceptual and strategic. If there was a shortcut, I was determined to find it, or make one up. If the choice was between learning a tactical approach and devising my own method, I'd choose to struggle on my own most of the time. I got along well with people who were philosophical, artistic, and entrepreneurial, but not those who were linear, deliberate, and detail oriented. The very people who I couldn't fathom at one time—physicists and engineers—would become clients and friends years later, to my great benefit, but not until I understood my own thinking. I had to think about *that*, and fortunately a teacher appeared to help.

My life was changed by a math teacher, Dorothy Sulock, who paid attention to what I was naturally good at (language) and helped me create a cognitive bridge that linked my preference for words to math concepts. She explained probability, for example, with a simple illustration using red balls and white balls in an opaque container. If you have so many red balls and an unequal number of white balls, how can you express the likelihood of removing a red one? She used words and symbols to explain the problem, but if people didn't understand, she'd say it another way, over and over, as many times as necessary. A gifted storyteller, she not only helped me learn math, but she also helped me become a conscious learner. I started to think about how I learn and process information in a way that I carried to graduate school and through advanced statistics.

While an undergrad, I hit a snag in statistics. Instead of struggling in silence, I met with my professor, Dr. Tracy Brown. I had managed to impress him by being the only student who had ever solved a particular riddle, and he was pretty bowled over. I realized later that he deduced from my ability to solve the riddle that words were my best tool. He encouraged me to think of the formulas not as symbols but as a way to analyze data in order to test an idea. His coaching helped me find a different approach, a tactic. But, his intervention was strategic—he was willing to look for an approach that I could understand, not by trying out one tactic or another but by being focused on the outcome. In other words, he looked at *what* first and *how* second.

## Blinded by Success

Once they have established a strategic direction and developed the tactics to move toward it, leaders need measures to evaluate progress. This isn't news. However, what can happen, quite unintentionally, is that particular methods, when they show success, become reified.

People in organizations develop a sense of identity that is about their role and the methods they use more than it is about the success or challenges of the entire entity. Leaders emotionally "marry" their methods, and leadership teams, including boards of directors, can become ossified in their thinking. Ironically, this is more likely when the organization is successful. This cognitive trap is called outcome bias, and we hear it loud and clear when people say things like, "If it ain't broke don't fix it," or, "Don't argue with success."[4]

What if the leaders of Wells Fargo had looked into the causes of the company's startling success? Wells Fargo's results in its retail banks were far better than those of its peer group, yet the top leaders didn't investigate. What if the leaders at Wells Fargo had used reversal? Reversal is the process of assuming an opposite point of view, and it can be done as a means to see something in a completely new way. When done for the sake of inquiry or learning, it is a marvelous tool.

Scrutinizing success needn't always be grounded in cynicism. Studying what makes a person or organization successful is a way to learn about the processes that led to the results. However, leaders may be leery of looking too closely, lest they discover that luck played a role. But realizing that fortune smiled upon a person or company is far better than believing that the tactics of an initiative are so genius that they must never be questioned.

Leaders who remain deeply curious about what is right in front of them are far better at avoiding the pitfalls of being stuck in either strategic or tactical thinking. Rather, they use their ability to think about thinking, recognize where their focus is, and ask, "When was the last time I looked at this differently?"

## REVERSAL IN PRACTICE

Here are some simple sample questions that promote the process of reversal:

- What if the best time to go on vacation in Europe is winter, not summer?

- What if we can bring the doctors to the patients?

- What if the information we are so happy about is a bad sign?

- What if the board should be setting metrics for management, instead of management telling the board how to evaluate progress?

# PART II

# EMOTIONAL REGULATION

**A**S IMPORTANT as intellect is for great leadership, it comes to little when emotion is denied. It is impossible to quash emotion, and much harm comes from ignoring it in ourselves or others. Great leaders are capable of using sensation (the biological experience we call feelings) as information. It turns out that knowing what we are feeling and understanding why (at least in part) can help us see many more options than if we slam the door on them. Great leaders appreciate the multiple factors influencing themselves and others, and, while avoiding simplistic interpretation, this awareness allows understanding and opens the door to empathy.

4

# To Be Analytical or to Be Creative Is Not Destiny

———————

Organizations clamor for creativity but too
often kill it with analysis. Imagination is the oxygen
of creativity, and it dies when constrained.
Leaders want "imagineers"—people who
merge creativity with pragmatism in real time,
lest the leader feel loss of control.

TWO GROUPS of people who can quickly push each other to the edge of reason are those who identify as analytical and those who identify as creative. Since our skills tend to line up with our jobs, analytical people tend to be in roles where they use systematic methods to understand data. They are often quite good at and enjoy logical processes, which they use to draw conclusions. Creative people may take in information in big gulps and see patterns based on grouping information in conceptual categories. They can be good at inferential leaps and symbolic thinking, whether expressed in words, music, painting, and so on.

My friend Ayse Birsel is an award-winning designer who has worked with companies such as GE, Herman Miller, Johnson & Johnson, Target, and TOTO. She and her husband, Bibi Seck, founded Birsel+Seck, and they live in New York City and Istanbul. Birsel exemplifies how to use dichotomies to create something new, opening herself to consider multiple options and opportunities before making a decision. A designer and businesswoman, she is creative *and* pragmatic, evidenced by her work. She can dream—and then turn around and analyze what it will take to make the dream come true. Her book *Design the Life You Love* guides the reader to dream and then deconstruct and reconstruct.[1] This is both a creative process and an analytical one.

Birsel's process is grounded in deep wisdom. A dream may be lovely and inspiring, but without deconstructing it to identify the elements and reconstructing it to create something new, it is a wish. But creation of the future we desire, whether as an individual or as a multi-billion-dollar company, requires more than analysis and methodology—it needs a motivating destination. The means to achieve something is no guarantee that anything useful or inspiring will be created.

When I met Birsel in New York, I was captivated by her charm, as anyone who meets her is. She spoke to a small mastermind group I was part of, and as she talked, I realized she was a gentle guide, taking us back and forth between big ideas and the mechanics. Birsel taught us a process that started with imagining, thinking without limits, then deconstructing the idea or image we created. Her ideas were fluid and integrated; she evoked curiosity, enthusiasm, and a sense that her method was not just for her or her colleagues, but something useful to anyone who would take the steps. Birsel was inviting us to think creatively *and* analytically, though she didn't use those words.

In stark contrast, some leaders fan the flames of black-and-white thinking, emphasizing differences and making it clear who and what they prefer. When leaders speak of people in terms of characteristics such as "analytical" or "creative" with even a hint of disdain, they create an environment where people are more likely to take sides, as if in a grown-up version of Red Rover. Even self-effacing comments, intended to reduce distinctions, merely reinforce differences. One executive I worked with, Phil, had been labeled "non-professional" early in his career because he didn't have the same academic background as most of his peers. He repeated this so often that, instead of making him "one of the gang" by showing humility, his words simply reinforced a distinction that wasn't helpful. True, he didn't have an advanced degree in a technical field, but he was as capable as anyone in the company who did. Once he stopped making fun of himself, his wickedly shrewd business head and great ability to see and appreciate talent in nearly everyone shined through. Phil's capacity to see and value analytical and creative talent eventually made him an extraordinarily influential leader. Among his peers, Phil stood out in his ability to see what was really going on and make decisions accordingly.

## Emotional Overload

But don't people have preferences, and aren't leaders people? Yes, and the job of leaders isn't to indulge their preferences; rather, it is to create an environment for people to perform and thrive while working toward common goals. It's a big job, and unless a leader is gifted with an open, nonjudgmental mind and very calm nervous system, they will have much to learn—about others, but importantly, about themselves. For example, leaders can be astonished that even casual comments can have major consequences and that words spoken out of anger or frustration can be devastating. In a crisis, a time when leaders need to be both creative and analytical, the situation can be so draining that there is insufficient energy to manage oneself. This may be what happened to Tony Hayward, CEO of British Petroleum, at the time of that deadly explosion on an oil rig in the Gulf of Mexico, described in Chapter 1. Understandably upset and exhausted, Hayward's infamous words about wanting his life back almost certainly show he was overcome by emotion. Indeed, emotion can overwhelm our best intentions, no matter how analytical or how in control we think we are.

In a crisis, leaders are tempted and probably encouraged to act quickly and decisively, use facts, and get out in front, to "lean in." This advice puts even more pressure on a leader and may increase the likelihood of big mistakes. My advice is to "lean back." Unless an emergency is so great that even thirty minutes matters, leaders should push away from the barrage of information, some of which is bound to be inaccurate, and think. Step away, mentally, to see if, as with the kaleidoscope, the pieces fall together differently, and assess the context. A few minutes of calm thinking are worth a fortune if they help a leader avoid a big mistake.

People do seem to be either more analytical than creative or vice versa, but these are tendencies, not destiny. Unfortunately, with the notion that such attributes are hardwired into our brains, we have taken up a narrow, and probably incorrect, position. The whole notion of "hardwired" when it comes to the human brain is, itself, a dubious construct. Our brains are not, after all, computers. While it's true that some behaviors are innate, including reflexes (a puff of air directed at our eyes will make us blink), the metaphor that more accurately represents our brains, brilliantly described in David Eagleman's book *Livewired: The Inside Story of the Ever-Changing Brain*, is a network.[2]

What makes us cling to the categories we use to understand others, and ourselves? Identity and threats to it. A tendency, talent, college major, job title, and so on can become everything. Once an aspect of identity is adopted, it's hard to shake, even if it creates limits. Why isn't it a simple matter of using rational thinking to manage conflicting information? Because doing so is difficult. Making sense of what seems disparate takes energy and can be annoying, and making rapid judgments allows us to sidestep the struggle with discomfort.

Our world is complicated, and often we must rely on representations of facts and statements of probability. How soon we forget that our best efforts are mere proxies, though the best we can come up with, and our predictions, even if usually right, aren't without fallibility.

"The first principle
is that you must not
fool yourself—and
you are the easiest
person to fool."

RICHARD FEYNMAN

## How We Think Is Who We Are—Or Is It?

While I was working to help a client with an acquisition, I met and got to know the executive leadership team of the acquired company. To use a broad category as a description, the new company was populated with cowboys who had just been acquired by gentlemen ranchers. This is a cartoonishly narrow view of each, akin to caricatures. I wouldn't normally use these descriptions, except it is a mostly accurate representation of how they reacted to one another.

The cowboys had built a thriving business from nothing and were now cashing in their chips, as founder/entrepreneurs often do. The limitation of founders is, sometimes, that they have a narrow base of experience, but from where they stand, they can't recognize that. Daniel Kahneman calls this the trap of believing "that powerful WYSIATI rule," which stands for "What You See Is All There Is."[3] That is how I described it to the executive from the acquiring company. Success is wonderful, but it can also be blinding.[4]

One day, I met with the head of the risk department of the newly acquired company. John was overtly hostile to me, seeing me as an agent of the other team, and he often muttered snarky comments that were overheard by many. Now I was alone with this man in his office, only to gather some background information, nothing more. That said, he was quite right that I'm always taking in more than what people deliberately communicate. I'm building an understanding of the person speaking. I'm absolutely not psychic, but sometimes people are afraid of me, as they are many consultants and especially psychologists.

John was visibly anxious, ready to defend himself. I asked him to explain their process, at a high level, for evaluating the risk of a given potential customer. I knew that this company was quite skilled at managing risk and that their account representatives were part of the reason why. They were very good observers of what many would not notice in a customer's place of business. They noted qualities like poorly maintained offices, inadequate staffing, and overgrown landscaping, and they closely scrutinized customers who were displaying signs of struggle—well before their difficulties showed up in missed payments. I was fascinated by the skill of the account representatives and, since some were far better than the others, was exploring how to codify what the great ones were doing so it could be taught and, perhaps, incorporated into how the broader company thought about risk. As I explained this idea to John, he became enraged. He stood up, slammed his hands on the desk, leaned over in red-faced rage, and screamed at me, "We don't use speculation to manage risk! We use analytics!"

Take just a moment to think about John. He was right that the company had superb data and analytics about potential customers, and even more and better about active customers. Still, some of their account managers had uncommonly low losses in their parts of the business. John wasn't interested in understanding how they achieved such good results, chalking them up to luck. He saw no irony in his lack of curiosity about the differences across the account managers. A lack of curiosity about unusual results, whether they be good or bad, is a risk. Sometimes people, like John, take too much comfort in analytical tools. Consistent results, over time, comfort many, even those who pride themselves on rational thinking and intellectual rigor. And we can be surprisingly threatened when events or other people call into question our methods, beliefs, or identity.

The trouble starts when people feel that they are either one way or the other, and that their way is best. When confronted with new information, even intelligent people can cling to what they already believe to be true. This is especially true if contradictory information is derived from unfamiliar methods, in which case the method itself may be dismissed, usually followed by discounting the person who used it and, thus, is presenting new information.

John Maynard Keynes rightly said, "The difficulty lies, not in the new ideas, but in escaping from the old ones."[5]

"The difficulty," as Keynes calls it, arises not only in the face of new ideas but also when our identity is challenged. People may exhibit discomfort in various ways, from subtle behaviors such as avoiding specific tasks or people to overt behaviors like becoming argumentative or aggressive. A simple example is that an artistic person who needs to do administrative duties may put off doing the work or deliberately delay, even knowing it will cause problems for others. An analytical person may be skeptical of methods that use words and imagery rather than numbers and code, even if doing so would produce a better result.

Knowing you have a particular strength, being proud of it, and using it flexibly requires adaptation. People who strongly identify with a characteristic—being analytical, for example—but who aren't adaptable will find success in some situations but will belly flop in others. Unfortunately, those with an inflexible identity often have a tendency to harshly judge people who are unlike them. People who are unable or unwilling to simply notice differences can be shockingly defensive and even aggressive when they feel judged, despite their tendency to be judgmental. Therefore, describing black-and-white thinking as purely cognitive is inaccurate. The ideas can certainly be in our minds, but the defensiveness, hostility, and harsh judgments of people who are seen as opposite are raw emotions.

Ayse Birsel's ability to bring her extraordinary creativity to what might appear to be problems of engineering is an example of meta-leadership. Conversely, John's inability to learn, except through methods he found acceptable, coupled with emotional outbursts show the powerful effect of emotion on thinking and behavior. Eventually, John lost his job, though many of his colleagues said it took far too long.

## A Different Look at Creativity

When Drew Madsen became president of Olive Garden restaurants, he had the challenges you would expect anyone taking the top job would face. He had an additional challenge, however. Prior to assuming the role of president, he had been the leader of marketing, but the majority of people at Olive Garden worked in operations. How would Madsen gain credibility with the thousands of people who prepared and served food to millions of guests? He hadn't climbed the ranks from working in a restaurant to managing a region to a senior executive role, and lots of people knew it.

Likewise, Carol Tomé's appointment as CEO of United Parcel Service marked the first time the company would be led by a woman and the first time the chief executive was chosen from outside the ranks of UPS executives. The task of any new CEO or president, Tomé included, isn't to persuade people that they are smart. It's to demonstrate that they understand the work that people do, no matter their jobs.

Tomé and Madsen have something in common that served them well—the ability to show genuine curiosity about what people do to keep the trains running on the right track. Tomé had a long and admirable career at The Home Depot and could speak with credibility about retail operations. Early in her time at UPS, she made sure to get out of the corporate office and into warehouses so she could see for herself what was happening. Madsen visited restaurants, dozens of them. He didn't just breeze through or sit and eat pasta, he asked questions and listened to the answers. Madsen and Tomé showed uncommon curiosity and sincerity, like the best leaders do when they take on a new role. Lilicia Bailey, chief human resources officer at Emory Healthcare, earned great credibility by seeking opportunities to learn about the institution that lay outside of her office. Early in her work in healthcare, she observed a surgery, something people talked about for a long time with great admiration.

# People who aren't adaptable will find success in some situations but will belly flop in others.

———

Madsen had a steep hill to climb early in his tenure. The leaders in operations took a "wait and see" attitude, expecting him to lead from the corporate office, using spreadsheets and monthly updates as a proxy for understanding what really goes on in a restaurant. However, less than two weeks into his tour, the operations leaders had a very different view. They were impressed by his earnest and low-key style and especially by his willingness to let others teach him—in front of whomever happened to be standing there!

If Madsen, Tomé, or Bailey had been unwilling to learn through creative means, not just by analyzing data and reports, it is very likely that their reputations would have been something like "another corporate type, come to tell us how to do our jobs." Unfortunately, it is a trap to think that leaders can learn everything they need to know from their office, by ceremonial visits to "the field," or in the back-to-back-to-back meetings that crowd so many calendars. Great leaders know that creativity is as essential as analysis to their ability to think strategically. The fuel for creativity is curiosity.

Failure to show sincere curiosity says, "I know everything, and you have nothing to tell me." It also tells people on the front lines that the job they do is important but they aren't. This is not the message you want to send to the thousands of people who look your customers in the eye every day, who speak to them, serve them, and create their view of your company.

Madsen took a risk by putting himself out there in front of his people in a vulnerable way, and he gained credibility as a result. Hundreds of people employed at Olive Garden restaurants felt they got to know him, and they liked his willingness to listen and learn. He showed his desire to learn the most basic things, *in public*. When a leader is sincerely curious, others are more likely to share what they know, and, in the process, both parties learn about each other as human beings.

As president, Madsen led the company to consistent same-store sales growth, a difficult feat in any business. The time and energy he invested in location after location, speaking with people in every job, was invaluable not only because he learned. His effort also sent employees in the restaurants the message that they are important, that what they do matters.

## The Brilliance of Both

People sometimes waste a lot of time and energy defending their preferences, especially when these are closely tied to identity. The greater the actual or perceived threat to identity, the more extreme the response. As Dr. Joanne Irving, a clinical psychologist and consultant, says, "People are the most dangerous when they are the most threatened."[6] How do we avoid provoking a response from another that will reduce the chance of a productive conversation, never mind a good working relationship, when we see ourselves as very different from that person? A remark on the painfully obvious, such as, "Well, you are clearly a creative," could be received as a compliment, as derogatory, or, perhaps most insulting, as our being too lazy to get to know another or thinking they aren't worth our interest.

As exemplified by Birsel and Madsen, meta-leaders do three things to mitigate the human tendency to think in dualities:

1 They remain alert to their own tendency to think in black and white, and they enlist others to help them when they don't realize they are falling into the trap. In short, they use meta-cognition *and* they accept their own fallibility.

2 They may use dualistic categories as descriptors but do not mistake these for the whole truth.

3 They do not allow people to describe others in derogatory or dismissive ways.

The first point, avoiding the dichotomy trap, is the hardest of the three. Richard Feynman, Nobel Prize winner in physics, wisely noted,

"The first principle is that you must not fool yourself—and you are the easiest person to fool."[7] Intelligence does not make us immune to delusional thinking or misguided beliefs, and since we are inevitably working with limited information, we succumb to "What You See Is All There Is." This is precisely why we need people around us whose judgment we can trust when we can't necessarily trust our own. In times of great ambiguity or high risk, or both, it's good to have someone who isn't in the eye of the storm with us. Proximity to an issue leads to particular perspectives, and when a point of view is shared by a group, it tends to be stronger. Collective expertise combined with common perspective can lead to great calamity.

Despite the number of brilliant engineers and scientists who work in the space program, sometimes disasters happen, like the explosion of the space shuttle *Challenger* in 1986. While serving on the Rogers Commission investigating the explosion, Feynman was highly critical of the decision to launch the rocket for a number of reasons, not only that he demonstrated that an O-ring at freezing temperature (or near freezing after sitting in a glass of ice water) was no longer pliable. If only Feynman had been available on launch day, he might have asked a few critical questions and illuminated a crucial risk.

Second, good leaders don't discount the importance and power of identity as a creative or analytical person, but they also don't buy the idea that we are all one or the other. A person can be creative *and* analytical. Unfortunately, in an effort to categorize people into "types," some organizations go so far as to add personality test results to office name plates, inviting everyone to take shortcuts in getting to know their colleagues, as though a score on a questionnaire is the person. This is an example of subrogation, a cognitive mistake in which a measure of something, no matter how weak, replaces the thing itself. Even though no smart people would say that a map of Italy is Italy, they will happily use erroneous measures of concepts only weakly related to organizational performance.

Third, leaders stop others from referring to people by a label unless it is a description of a relationship or behavior. "Customer," for example, indicates a relationship, and "key customer" describes how the customer and the business interact.

## Dreaming with Our Feet on the Ground

Big ideas can be dismissed as delusions, and sometimes they are. But we are living with everyday comforts and tools that mere decades ago didn't exist. In the comic strip *Dick Tracy*, some of the characters wore communication devices like wrist watches. In the early to mid-twentieth century, the average person thought it a pipe dream, but now devices that can be worn like a timepiece literally connect us to the world. News that previously took days to transmit is available in seconds. When the idea for computers for home use was first introduced by science fiction writer Arthur C. Clarke on the Australian Broadcasting Corporation program *Perspective* in 1974, many thought it a fantastical notion. If we don't use our minds to analyze the steps from our current reality to one that is predicted, imagine how easily we might dismiss big ideas. Conversely, when analysis tells us that something is improbable or impossible, sometimes we persist past all reason.

Leaders can help themselves and others to employ both creativity and analysis, first by engaging in both themselves. They can learn to dream with their feet on the ground.

## HOW TO DREAM WITH YOUR FEET ON THE GROUND

To engage analytical and creative aspects from a meta-perspective, do the following:

1  Visualize your ideal future.

2  Analyze your vision.

3  Choose two or three elements of the vision you will pursue.

4  Look at your environment. What and who can help you create what you have in mind? What or who is an impediment to moving in the direction you want to go?

5  Reflect on your process—think about your thinking. Notice what is exciting, annoying, or scary.

5

# The Fallacy of Absolute Courage and Total Cowardice

We mistake courage and cowardice for
fixed, inborn traits, but behavior is
also shaped by the situation, over which
leaders have power.

COURAGE AND COWARDICE are often thought of as elements of character, inborn qualities that a person either has or doesn't have. Courageous people do what needs to be done, even at personal risk, while cowards hide in the shadows, make excuses, and can't be honest with even themselves. If you take a moment to think of images of courageous and cowardly people, you will likely envision characters who are at the extreme, perhaps even cartoonish. Even though you know the images are too simple, they are easy to conjure, which tells us how embedded they are in our collective thinking.

I encountered real-life examples of the most cartoonish versions of courage and cowardice while leading a workshop for accounting professionals. One of the people in the class—I've deleted his name from memory, but let's call him Joe—took up the role of devil's advocate. It was clear from the start that Joe had some power in the group. He had a strong presence, sat very straight, and was tall enough that he was hard to miss. While I spoke, he occasionally interrupted me and asked questions, mostly relevant. Toward the end, he attacked my profession and me personally. The room was silent as people stared at their fingernails. I asked Joe if he was challenging my competence, and he said, "No, I'm just asking questions that no one else is brave enough to ask."

In the same workshop, Cynthia sat mostly silent for two hours and asked only a single question. However, she was listening intently and afterward approached me to talk about Joe, her colleague who had been so combative. She felt like a coward for not speaking up but knew doing so wouldn't end well.

Cynthia was concerned about her career because her colleague was highly regarded in the firm, while she'd received feedback about being "meek." I said I thought she had good judgment but might be in the wrong environment. Yes, she might work to be braver and more forthright, but if she was going to get slammed for her attempts, why should she? Asking people to be courageous but not making it safe to do so is like asking people to subject themselves to punishment to show how tough and dedicated they are. It's just foolish. Allowing brutish behavior and justifying it as "bold and courageous" is abdication of leadership, but it happens.

Great leaders understand that words matter, and they don't accept labels as a proxy for knowledge. Leadership, done well, recognizes the emotion attached to language and behavior and checks to see what systemic forces are contributing to dynamics. This is the essence of the emotional aspect of meta-leadership.

## Courage and Cowardice— Not What We Think

As with all dichotomies, the desire to simplify and be quick about it leads us to draw faulty conclusions. John D. Norton, distinguished professor of history and philosophy of science at the University of Pittsburgh, writes, "The measured deliberations of cautious scholars are no match for the popular demand for simple answers."[1]

Courageous people are bold and decisive, have no fear, and may be impervious to pain, while cowards are sniveling, insecure, indecisive, and overwhelmed by emotion. These stereotypes are often associated with high-stakes situations that involve personal risk, such as plane crashes, an explosion on an oil rig, wars, political turmoil, or a global pandemic. We expect conformity to our criteria for courage and judge harshly those leaders who stumble.

Our tendency to orient toward drama, in part because it is so vivid, can obscure everyday courage or cowardice, even in ourselves. Dr. Jim Detert's research, captured in his book *Choosing Courage*, shows us that courage isn't a quality we either have or don't have; it can be developed.[2] But too often our attempts to be courageous are unrealistically ambitious. He points out that we are at risk when we embark on something new because we won't be great at it right away. We might look incompetent or uncertain because we genuinely don't know how to do what we are trying to learn. If we start a business but have never done that before, how could we know what it will be like? We don't, yet we fear appearing incapable even if the only way we could be capable is through magic. Most people have an aversion to appearing weak or incapable, and it's not hard to see why. Detert's work points out that people do want to learn but don't want to look foolish in the process. Fear of learning in front of others stops some people from trying or makes it difficult to accept critique if they do attempt new things. The fear of looking bad makes some people give up rather than allow others to see imperfection. However, Detert emphasizes the value of showing vulnerability. Doing so is humanizing. He says that, especially for men, for people who are assertive, or for people who are extremely rational and perhaps cold, allowing others to see some struggle can inspire respect and even loyalty.

Detert's work has profound importance for leaders, but also for anyone who has influence or authority. He quite rightly takes courage out of the realm of myth and debunks the idea that you either have it or you don't by talking about courageous behavior. His research gives us a pragmatic way to think about courage using behavioral science.

## Fear of Looking Like a Coward
## Diminishes Courage

In the television series *Downton Abbey*, the cook, Mrs. Patmore, is saddened to learn that her nephew, Archie, a soldier during World War I, is missing.[3] After a short time, she learns that he has died, though not from wounds inflicted by adversaries. Instead, he was shot for cowardice. It's a wrenching scene when she hears the news, but the saga doesn't end there. Later, when many villages are erecting statues and laying plaques for the fallen soldiers, Mrs. Patmore finds out that her nephew's name will be excluded from public acknowledgment in his home village. The character's reaction is beautifully written to encompass grief at the loss of her nephew, shame that he was branded a coward, and fear of being judged by others should they find out.

The situation in the TV show is resolved when Archie is named in a special memorial in Downton. Lord Grantham realizes the village could know about Archie—that he volunteered to serve and died during the war—without exposing his cook or himself to the scorn that may have come if the whole story were told. This public display is essential to the story. Still, the more significant element is that Lord Grantham did not leap to a predictable response, to heap criticism on the deceased soldier, as many viewers probably suspected he would. I did. But, I was more interested in how the story unfolded in such a way as to acknowledge the complexity of a character who would volunteer for service, then later abandon his unit. Was Archie courageous at one time and cowardly at another?

The storyline in *Downton Abbey* shows us the power of context to influence behavior, even when we believe that character is fixed and predicts behavior. This idea is false. Character gives us information about tendencies, but circumstances will have their say. However, it's simpler to think that people's behavior will match their character in all situations.

"You develop the skills to act competently in courageous situations by practicing those skills regularly."

———————

**JIM DETERT**

An important variable is emotion, especially fear, which creates noise and interferes with the ability to see clearly. Fear, whether experienced consciously or not, can distract even smart leaders. A leader who is concerned that they may not be acting boldly enough tends to do one of two things: stick with the status quo or act impulsively. These are different overt actions, but fear may be a common factor. Each is a shortcut, and each serves to rid the leader of unpleasant emotion, though many leaders would vociferously deny they would follow either course of action. Conveniently, rationalizations are available for most situations, but they come at a cost because they obscure what is really going on.

My clients know that I am not shy about giving advice; of course, I've been invited and paid to do so. Often, I see things differently than they do, which leads to great discussions, but sometimes my advice shocks them into silence. This happens most commonly in three scenarios: (1) during a crisis of some sort; (2) when faced with a high-stakes decision such as strategic direction or a merger or acquisition; and (3) after a long period of success that is showing signs of softness. Leaders tend to exhibit boldness in the first two situations and far less in the third. Why? When there is a crisis, people are watching, and pending high-stakes decisions become known, at least by insiders.

I advised one CEO, Paul, to replace his chief financial officer, who had embarrassed him in front of the board. Paul wasn't listening until I told him that the board would not complain about his CFO more than once. The next conversation would be about his judgment in keeping a CFO who wasn't performing. Fortunately, Paul rethought his decision. Later, the board chair revealed to me and to Paul that he had been prepared to demand the change of CFO, a move he felt would undermine Paul as the CEO and damage their relationship.

Leaders can ill afford to look like they don't know what they are doing, but sometimes the urgency to act and desire to appear decisive leads to:

- relying on irrelevant data;
- failing to ask for the right kind of help;
- listening to sycophants; or
- overvaluing consistency at the expense of accuracy.

Why do intelligent leaders do these things? Fear. Fear of criticism, fear of losing support, fear of falling out of favor with the board and investors, fear of losing status, fear of being accused of inconsistency, and reasons I'm sure you can add from your observations.

Unexamined fear is a hidden cause of many questionable actions. Here are a few examples:

- One board came within twenty-four hours of firing their CEO based on a rumor that turned out to be unfounded.

- A floundering president ordered the CFO to "jiggle" the sales numbers to be more favorable.

- A division president moved an underperforming vice-president from job to job for more than ten years before her boss gave the ultimatum to fire the VP or he would remove her.

Fear is a normal feeling when there is a threat, large or small, and it can be a vital clue that something is amiss. Great leaders don't simply dismiss fear, they examine it, talk to others whom they trust, and decide about what to do and what they aren't willing to do.

## The Courage to Be Bad at Something

Dr. Frances Frei is a professor at Harvard Business School, co-author of *Uncommon Service*, and creator of a popular TED Talk.[4] One bit of advice she writes about is choosing what to be bad at. Frei says that when people or companies don't prioritize, they are set up to fail. No one person and no company can be excellent at everything, though many fail rather than make an informed decision about what matters least to their ideal customers. Failure to make this critical decision does not lead to excellence; instead, it guides individuals and companies to spread resources too thin and disappoint on numerous fronts. On an individual level, failing to cull the list of "must-dos" leads to exhaustion and a sense of failure, even when a superhuman effort is expended.[5]

While Frei was explaining this concept to me, my mind was racing ahead to imagine how my clients would react to this advice. I was ready to bet that it would be met with resistance. That's a mild version of what I was envisioning. I asked Frei if her clients pushed back on this advice, and she said, "Oh, yes!" Quick, defensive reactions are emotional, no matter how intellectualized they are. But knowing this is far from enough, because once a strong emotional response shows up, it influences us more than we want to or will admit.

Naturally, Frei is ready for this reaction from leaders, and I was eager to hear how she handles it. After the client says, "I have to be good at everything. It's all important," she asks them if they are currently good at everything. But, of course, no one is good at everything. The question is not, "Are you bad at something?" The question is, "Are you selecting what to be bad at?" Usually, the weak parts of an organization are so by default, not because of a strategic decision. The same is true for individuals who try to be "superhuman" and are mediocre at most things instead.

When I was a stockbroker, my colleagues were mostly men, but I was fortunate to have two women peers. Each of us had a husband and children, and each felt overwhelmed. One consciously decided to be "okay" as a broker, one hired a full-time housekeeper, and I tried to do it all. It was a mistake. I was exhausted. Even though my female colleagues wanted to reassure me that they felt inadequate in virtually every area of their lives, I kept trying to be a superwoman. Following Frei's advice would have been convenient then. I was awash in negative feelings about myself but kept trying to put on a good face. Fortunately, I could pivot, a move that got me on the right path.

## Strategic Patience

In my misery about my job as a broker, I found it hard to think straight about what to do next, so I regularly escaped to a bookstore. A couple of times each week, I would leave the office; no one cared if you were there or not, and, if you weren't there, gossiping about you was that much easier. My conscious plan was to figure out why my clients, most of whom were professional people with a lot of education, made foolish decisions about their money. To substantiate this claim about my clients, here are a few examples:

- One woman, in her sixties, wanted to sell all her investments and "loan" the cash to her son-in-law to open a retail store.

- A college professor, believing he had found the secret to investment success, was trading options with his retirement savings and ended up losing a third of his money.

- A very wealthy client, trading on margin, panicked when the markets significantly downturned and locked in substantial losses. He sued the firm, and his personal life crumbled.

At the same time, I felt like a coward for lacking the courage to quit this job I hated and get out of an extremely hostile working environment. I'm not naming the firm because it matters little. The others were no better. I know this because I practiced interviewing at the brokerage firms I wasn't interested in to learn what they looked for in new hires. In hindsight, my self-criticism about being a coward was blocking my ability to see that what I was doing was brave. Later,

# Blaming others, or ourselves, for failure doesn't teach us how something happened.

———

I could see the dichotomy trap of courage and cowardice at play. I was afraid to quit my job, but while I was in it, I expended great effort to learn. I was afraid to complain, but I did raise my concerns with the office manager. His reply? "If you can't stand the heat, get out of the kitchen." After that, I began to plot my escape in earnest, though it would take months to execute.

Later, when advising senior executives, I could see similar behaviors in some. I began to refer to the essential aspect of managing the dichotomy of courage and cowardice as "strategic patience."

## From Deconstructing to Depersonalizing

The adage is that we learn a lot from failure, and I was taking that to heart as I planned to change my life. I began a process that I would later learn is deconstructing—reflecting on a situation by looking at its parts and how they fit together. Simply leaning back and thinking helps us avoid oversimplifying because we may feel less pressure to use shortcuts, such as default thinking. As I pondered my future, it helped to realize that getting a new job is easier when you already have one. I asked myself what I liked about being a stockbroker and what was untenable. I realized that certain aspects of my job were rewarding. Number one on the list was my clients; not all of them, but many. Some clients were good partners. They were honest, interested in my thoughts and advice, willing to learn, and engaged as partners. These relationships felt mature and mutually trusting. I was genuinely curious about why people made the choices they did and knew not only that I didn't know their methods, but that they didn't know either, and neither did my colleagues. When I tried to talk about this with colleagues, my questions were met with extreme disinterest and even scorn.

I discovered other things I liked: autonomy, a degree of professional regard (not universal, of course), satisfaction at being able to earn the necessary credentials, certainty of base pay (meager, but a safety net) and health insurance, and rewards such as bonuses, recognition, and additional training. What I didn't like was frat-boy behavior, blatant sexism, and open disrespect for clients. What I learned in hindsight was this:

- Systemic forces are powerful but, like rip currents, hard to see.

- Recognizing that a phenomenon is systemic doesn't mean we understand its power.

- People who aren't curious are dull companions, but when they are also domineering, they create fear in others.

The big lesson, which came years later, is that failure is less valuable if we personalize everything. People find it easier to judge and blame and harder to learn. Blaming others, or ourselves, doesn't teach us how something happened, but it does keep alive the obsession to find out who to blame. Knowing who is responsible is essential, and nefarious deeds need to be routed out, but equally important is understanding the context, and the systemic forces, to prevent repetition.

Fortunately, I did enough deconstructing to get me on a different path, one that would lead me to the right place. Later, I began to depersonalize my experience, take responsibility for myself, *and* recognize the forces at work that I could not influence.

## Fear of Looking Weak Makes Us Weaker

Identifying the systemic forces that support misdeeds doesn't absolve individuals. Still, it makes their behavior less mysterious and shows us why leaders can ill afford to ignore culture, no matter how much of a "soft" issue they believe it to be.

If, when deconstructing to understand what has happened, we look only at individuals or just the context, an incomplete picture will emerge. Leaders must push aside the belief that studying culture will mean that they don't hold people accountable for individual actions. Leaders may feel more pressure to find out who did what than to understand why and what factors played a part. The stress on a leader can be significant, but great leaders step back to enable them to see multiple factors; for example, individual, interpersonal, cultural, and so on. Deconstructing, especially when done deliberately and with discipline, is harder than it sounds but is more than worth the effort.

When Mary Barra became CEO of General Motors, she faced a crisis. GM was accused of hiding problems with some ignition switches, which had led to thirteen deaths. In addition, the National Highway Traffic Safety Administration declared that GM had used faulty switches for more than ten years even though they knew about the problem.

As with many situations, the problem was more significant than first thought. The company was threatened with lawsuits for over $10 billion, a staggering sum. Barra found out the technical reasons for the failures and wisely looked for reasons why they had been kept secret for so long. What sort of culture had developed that allowed it?

Barra searched for *what* caused GM employees to hide serious problems, not just for *who* did it. She could have blamed people for not having the courage to report it, but she wasn't simply looking for who to blame. When issues of wrongdoing occur, it is important to understand who was involved, of course. Leaders who investigate, blame, and punish may receive praise, and onlookers surely feel relieved. However, meta-leaders—like Barra, who realized the problems weren't just with individuals—look at systemic problems.

To return to the example of Wells Fargo, in 2016, when the Los Angeles city attorney's office publicly revealed that Wells Fargo employees had opened as many as two million bogus deposit and credit card accounts without the knowledge of its customers, the CEO, John Stumpf, admitted that he felt "accountable" for the transgressions but said that some employees didn't honor the bank's values.[6] Unfortunately, Stumpf utterly failed to look at the layers of management between himself and the customer-facing employees, preferring to take the "few bad apples" position—one that didn't hold water for long.

Less than two weeks after the issue became public, Stumpf appeared before the Senate Committee on Banking, but only later did frontline employees begin to report being pressured to engage in dishonest behavior. At a distance, it is easy to think people should have resisted the pressure. However, once more was revealed, we began to see how the employees felt no option but to comply.

## How to Build Courage

Years after my horrible experience at a brokerage firm and later while writing about courage in *High-Stakes Leadership*, I met Jim Detert at Thinkers50 in London. I was an attendee among this very august group of business thinkers, and Detert was a speaker. And what was he speaking about? Building courage. He presented his research findings, and to my great relief they supported what I'd been saying—that courage can be developed; it isn't a "you have it or you don't" character trait. Detert's book *Choosing Courage* is one every leader should read. It lays out multiple important concepts from his work, two of which I highlight here. Importantly, Detert gives the reader a generous supply of pragmatic advice about how to use his research.

First, courage can be developed. The late John Lewis recalled the work he and his colleagues did to prepare themselves to take nonviolent action against discrimination—because it doesn't come naturally to us to remain nonreactive when we are being physically harmed. Detert rightly connects the training of Lewis and his colleagues and military training to long-standing research in exposure therapy. This gradual process of experiencing what challenges us or makes us afraid, in greater and greater quantities over time, effectively builds skill and confidence in our ability to manage what we once avoided, rationalized away, or worked around.

A gradual approach makes intuitive sense. Yet, many people still think that failure in the most challenging situations is a sign of cowardice, and who among us doesn't shrink from that feeling? Sometimes, frustration with ourselves leads to impulsive behavior accompanied by declarations such as, "I have no fear." That is neither normal nor desirable. On this topic, Detert quotes M. Scott Peck, who said, "The absence of fear is not courage; the absence of fear is some kind of brain damage."[7]

Second, developing courage happens in context—the people around us matter. Confronting a bully at work to prove we are courageous is a fool's errand. Instead, we have to ask, "Why are bullies allowed to continue making others miserable?" Sometimes the cowards are the leaders who fail to address bad behavior, often because the bully delivers something desirable.

Harvard Business School professor Amy Edmondson's work on psychological safety illuminates the significant role of organizational culture in human behavior. Her research shows that people do not speak up, even if something is amiss, if they fear that they will be criticized, shamed, or punished for doing so.[8] Detert asserts that encouraging people to be courageous while ignoring a culture that makes it necessary to call on courage to do the most routine tasks is ineffective and bound to fail. He and Edmondson agree that leaders should create an environment where people can learn individually and collectively. As a result, people can tolerate and learn from mistakes, experiment, course-correct, and thrive in such organizations.

Decades of research show that leadership requires more than strategy and logical thinking. Leadership requires thinking *and* an understanding of emotion, especially the leader's emotions. Achieving the necessary knowledge of the role of our own emotions and default behaviors to improve leadership is a journey. Some may say it is the archetypal hero's journey.[9]

## LIVE LIKE AN EXPLORER, THINK LIKE A SCIENTIST

You can become more accustomed to the discomfort of learning in public by practicing the following:

1   Be an explorer in your territory. Put on your Indiana Jones hat and look around. Take note of how quickly your mind moves from observation to judgment. Now, once you notice how quickly you are making judgments, ask yourself if doing so keeps your a priori beliefs intact. In simple terms, does making quick judgments keep your feathers from being ruffled?

2   Pay attention to what and to whom you aren't giving attention. What leaders pay attention to and what they don't speaks volumes. For example, have you ever noticed that if you see a random person pointing up at the sky, people around them will almost always look to where they are pointing? How much more impactful is it when a leader "points"? It's enormous. Pay attention.

3   Make a list. Note who you are ignoring and ask yourself why that is. If you disregard people who make your work harder because they make you think, you are taking the easy way out. If you ignore people because they are chronically divisive for little gain, move them out.

4   Learn in public. If you, a leader, have been satisfied with know-
    ing only *what* but nothing about *how* or *why*, your organization
    will not learn quickly and innovate. Channel your inner four-
    year-old. Kids ask a lot of "why" questions, and so should you.

5   Ask questions when things are going well. If a leader doesn't
    know why things are happening or what the cause is, their
    judgments about what to do will be accidentally correct.
    Spectacular performance should be studied to learn and ensure
    that it's legit.

6

# Independent Decisions Always Depend On Something

Independence and dependence are temporary.
Interdependence allows us to rely on
others and ourselves in relation to circumstances.
Inflexible dependence or independence is
a trap, comforting though it may be.

ROBERT WAS AN imposing figure, tall with a swagger that reminded me of Steve McQueen. A serial entrepreneur, he grew a call-center business, Always-On, and decided to sell after accumulating substantial personal wealth. Although he loved the trappings of success, his true love was independence. His self-description was not surprising: "I'm good at starting up businesses and growing them fast, but I can't deal with bureaucracy and a bunch of corporate dependents, so I sell, make a lot of money, and start over."

If you walked into a room with Robert and his leadership team, you would have no trouble recognizing who was in charge. Robert was an intelligent opportunist masquerading as a sophisticated entrepreneur, and most everyone was either fooled or afraid. Thus, he encountered little resistance to his ideas. Robert was also skillful in selecting sycophants for top management roles. His primary criteria, more important than competence, was a person's willingness to agree with him. He rewarded his management team with lofty titles and generous bonuses, always entirely at his discretion. He communicated disdain for employees by isolating himself from them and allowing the office environment to remain unclean, inadequate, and dated. Despite conditions that would be unacceptable to most, the company was growing rapidly.

Seven years in, potential buyers were showing interest. Some wanted to enter a new industry, and others simply wanted to enlarge their footprint. Robert wanted a buyer who hadn't run a business like his, and he wanted to stay on as CEO. So, naturally, he planned to negotiate healthy compensation and bonus opportunities for himself. Then, Robert would retreat to his yacht, phone in orders to his loyal team, and contemplate his next move. He was fond of saying he wouldn't kowtow to the new owners or become a "dead-eyed corporate wonk."

The eventual buyer, we'll call them Springboard, was in a business related to Robert's. On paper, the deal looked great.

The president of Springboard, Randy, met with Robert over dinner. They spent two hours talking and ended with a handshake agreement. Randy admired Robert's entrepreneurial spirit, even if he was a bit of a "cowboy." However, Randy also knew that while Robert may be indispensable in the short run, he could be trouble long term. Looking across the dinner table at Randy, Robert saw an aging corporate executive, a "fat cat," with an overblown sense of his competence, and he wasn't entirely wrong. However, he was wrong about how far he could push Randy and for how long.

The stage was set for disaster, in part because they imagined one another as caricatures, the cowboy and the fat cat, oversimplified and inflexible versions of reality. They were both right, but only in broad strokes.

## The Unseen Fuel of Emotion

When people make rapid judgments, they do so with incomplete information. Depending on the complexity of the circumstance, less than the full picture may be enough. However, when a situation is uncertain, leaping to a conclusion is highly prone to error, though most are unwilling to admit it. People are incredibly likely to cling to their assessments, seeking confirmatory data and ignoring contradictory information. Robert and Randy were both maneuvering, each believing so strongly in their ability to act independently that they were unaware of the extent to which they were being taken in. This is precisely what Maria Konnikova's research shows.[1]

The massive body of research in behavioral economics rarely explores the role of emotion, except to mention it as a trap. In fairness, the researchers Daniel Kahneman, Dan Ariely, and Richard H. Thaler, to name just three, explore how humans make decisions; less so how they feel while making them and how the social context creates demands to behave one way or another. Nevertheless, Kahneman puts his finger on a critical feature of human thinking and decision-making, cognitive effort, and cognitive ease: exerting the effort for hard intellectual work demands energy and intention. Kahneman rightly points out that the hard work of deliberate thought is a lot less pleasant than leaping to conclusions, so human beings tend to make the effort only insofar as they believe it necessary. Of course, the tension between a desire to understand and the appeal of speed happens outside of our awareness, leaving plenty of room for mistakes.[2] Understanding that hard things require a different approach is helpful, but we might not be willing to admit, even to ourselves, that something is hard. Denial and overconfidence conspire to push rightful uncertainty to the side as though it is a nuisance rather than a worthy challenge.

The dinner meeting with Randy and Robert was high stakes, yet each was so distracted by his overwhelming need to show he was "large and in charge" that it distorted their views of each other. When people work hard to present a particular image, the effort narrows attention and leaves little space for curiosity. Think about a time when you were in a scary situation and how well you could pay attention to what someone said—it's hard. Binary thinking, oversimplifying, and seeing situations as either one thing or another eases the burden and reduces anxiety. It's understandable that people do this. After all, who wants to be maxed out on tension? The downside is that we don't see reality, but rather a distorted version of it, and our decisions afterward aren't as good.

For Randy and Robert, their quick characterizations of each other as a "fat cat" and a "cowboy" felt right, and the negotiations proceeded based on their beliefs. Neither of them leaned back to ask, "What evidence do I have?" Their thinking had been hijacked by the need to show independence and dominance—a default for both men. Likewise, each viewed the other as needing this deal, dependent upon it to achieve his objectives.

Robert was in no hurry to sell, but Randy was eager to buy, and the analysts on his team made a good case to acquire Robert's company. Indeed, their strategy made this potential acquisition very attractive, though Randy insisted he would walk away if he couldn't get what he wanted. However, Randy and his team weren't thinking about, nor did they understand, Robert's personal goal, which was to sell his company but be left alone to continue to run it. It's a familiar story in acquisitions, and the power of the dynamic is often underestimated, as it was in this case.

Soon after they finalized the deal, Randy's company sent an overseer to ease the transition from stand-alone start-up to part of a larger business. Stan, the leader chosen for the role, had a spotty track record and was in over his head. Robert viewed Stan as a "corporate leech," someone who was dependent on a big company to tell him what to do. Stan naively thought the exchange of funds for ownership would induce Robert to relinquish control.

Predictably, the tensions mounted as Robert insisted on independence while Stan pushed for him to realize he was now dependent. The clashes were obvious, and soon the business was headed in the wrong direction. It was a full-on, grown-up version of tug-of-war.

This example shows how a string of decisions, many made on autopilot, nearly led to a crash. The founder may not have been

"The difficulty
lies, not in the
new ideas, but
in escaping from
the old ones."

---

**JOHN MAYNARD KEYNES**

amenable to a cooperative approach in any case, but we'll never know. Instead, the acquiring company treated Robert like a commodity, a typical cowboy founder clinging to his independence while happily cashing a big check. Simultaneously, Robert's dim view of his new colleagues and boss was just as oversimplified and rigid. As a result, the opportunity to create a smooth glide path for the company was cut short, and after a tumultuous six months, Robert resigned under pressure. Unfortunately, the leadership team had already been treated to Robert's very dim view of the people from Springboard. Despite Robert's departure, the polarization continued, followed by the removal of most of the leadership team he had hired and a revolving door of presidents. By the time a competent leader was finally installed, years had passed and millions of dollars had gone down the drain.

Fortunately, a very good leader, Philip, was finally put in charge. Aware of the push-pull of dependence and independence, he forged a new course—one that helped people see the benefits of an interdependent relationship. He announced to the Always-On team new policies that directly and immediately improved their lives, such as better medical insurance and benefits for higher education, something they hadn't had before. Philip spent much of his time getting to know people beyond what job they held and, in the many conversations he had, could help individuals see how their particular situation was better because of Springboard. He also shaped a new narrative for his boss, supported by improved results, demonstrating to the top leaders at Springboard the value the acquired company was adding, and he set the company on a course that led to a more mature, profitable business.

## Dichotomies Distort

Despite the volume of research on decision-making, people still tend to overestimate how well they analyze a situation and underestimate the role of emotion in it.

In the case of the Always-On acquisition, emotion was not merely a factor; it played a more significant role than any of the parties realized. First, let's remember that the players in this saga were all intelligent and experienced businesspeople. Nothing they did was because of willful foolishness, but once they had extreme and fixed ideas of each other, they were locked in conflict. The distortions that became rampant in the case of Always-On were harsh judgments—some correct but others errors in thinking, fueled by the need for control, the need to be accurate, and the need to save face, to name a few.

Judgments can be extremely harsh when they have a moral undertone. For example, people are harsh judges when they believe others have selfish motives. Yet, ordinary people are, rightly, concerned about their self-interest but see no moral failing in it because they deem their motives purer. Righteous indignation can quickly fog the lens through which we look, even as we insist our decisions are for the common good.

Yet, organizations often praise and reward heroics, some of which aren't heroic, as well as other bandages on flawed processes. Rewarding heroics invites people to behave as martyrs, sacrificing their time, energy, and even relationships for the good of an organization that has become dependent on a few people to fill in where better processes should exist. Just as certainly, someone whose identity involves extreme self-sacrifice will fight tooth and nail to keep in place the systems that make their behavior advantageous and even essential.

Mutual dependencies keep people stuck in patterns that blind them to the downsides of what they are doing. A weak boss may depend on subordinates to compensate for qualities that he or she should possess—strategic thinking, for example. Instead, meta-leaders will recognize their weaknesses and improve on them, and will still invite others to give their ideas. In this way, great leaders move between dependence and independence, being stuck in neither. Great leaders know that independent thinking is critical to avoiding the hazards of groupthink, where the influence of a group leads to increased conformity and less rigorous discussion, laying the path for mistakes. They also understand that they cannot generate all ideas, methods, and solutions on their own.

## Factors That Influence Decisions

Why is it so difficult to prevent our feelings from influencing our decisions? The simple answer is, once again, because we are human. Factors like our temperament, family history, and socioeconomic status also influence our decision-making. Complicating the process further is that many of the factors that influence us are unconscious in nature. We cannot analyze every situation requiring a decision, and sometimes we don't need to. Vanilla or pistachio? No one would choose something they didn't like, so there's little downside even if they are wavering between good options. Also, you can always get both. Yet, even choices among pleasurable possibilities can be influenced by factors such as cultural identity. Imagine you are in an ice cream store, and you hear someone ask for the praline flavor. Where are they from? If you guessed the southern US, you might be right. Green tea ice cream? Likely the Pacific Northwest.[3]

We don't often think of choosing ice cream flavors as a dilemma, but most of us have been with a friend who agonized over the choices, only to order vanilla. One way to escape a dilemma is to default to familiar things, and those defaults sometimes reveal identity.

No harm, it's just ice cream.

Imagine that you were the person who noticed that people often ordered two flavors of ice cream, and that there wasn't a way to swirl two flavors together. Voila, the swirl machine! Both vanilla *and* chocolate. The ice cream innovation doesn't save lives, but it's fun and an example of wondering, thinking, and figuring out how to have both.

## Think Like a Scientist

Richard Feynman, the Nobel Prize–winning physicist who served on the Rogers Commission, which was charged with examining the explosion of the space shuttle *Challenger,* recounted some of the commission's work in his book *"What Do You Care What Other People Think?"*[4] Feynman was a young physicist during World War II and worked on developing the atomic bomb. Ever curious and somewhat mischievous, he noticed that the fence around the "high security" area where he worked had a hole. Feynman decided to test the astuteness of the security guards by exiting the facility through the hole, then re-entering past the guards who had seen him just a few minutes before. He was testing a hypothesis, which is what scientists, and great leaders, do. Feynman could have concluded that the security team was "asleep at the wheel" simply by noting the damaged fence, but rather than jumping to conclusions, he tested his idea. Unfortunately, he discovered the guards were even less aware than he suspected. It took multiple re-entries into the facility before the guards noticed he was entering but not leaving, or so they thought.

Feynman's example of independent thinking *and* dependence on a disciplined process—the scientific method of testing a hypothesis—is useful for business leaders. Processes and rules about how to get things done are necessary. Even a small business must rely on known methods to acquire inventory, hire people, collect money, and pay what's owed. What Feynman shows us is we cannot assume merely because a process exists and is familiar that it is effective.

During Feynman's work on the Rogers Commission, Morton Thiokol—the defense-contracting firm that built the solid-fuel booster rockets and a critical part, the O-rings—became the focus of inquiry. Relying on disciplined thinking rather than succumbing to groupthink, Feynman found himself in conflict with the others on the commission.

The O-rings were known to not perform as expected in freezing temperatures, but on January 28, 1986, with a crew having worked through the night to clear the vehicle of ice, and with ice all over the launch pad, the decision was to launch, with catastrophic results. What led to the decision? The urgency to launch and reliance on past success even when technical data identified risk are two reasons. Human errors. The commission finally issued its report and said

> Failures in communication ... resulted in a decision to launch 51-L based on incomplete and sometimes misleading information, a conflict between engineering data and management judgments, and a NASA management structure that permitted internal flight safety problems to bypass key Shuttle managers.[5]

Feynman was so dissatisfied with the report of the Presidential Commission on the Space Shuttle *Challenger* Accident that he threatened not to sign it. Only when he was allowed to write an appendix, recounting his observations, did he relent. Known as Appendix F, it is a stunning and precise piece of writing. Writes Feynman in the appendix, "For a successful technology, reality must take precedence over public relations, for nature cannot be fooled."[6]

Feynman's comments are hard to argue with, but time and again leaders are tempted to save face or avoid criticism by telling half-truths, feigning ignorance, or lying. When misdeeds are discovered, criticism is not usually long in coming and can be vicious. People ask, with real or dramatized incredulity: How could the leader do that? How could they let that happen? Why were they so dependent on bad advice?

Leaders function in a social context, as does everyone who isn't a hermit. Your thoughts, opinions, and decisions are influenced by others—what they think and what you predict they might think, say, or do based on your actions. Meta-leadership is a way of seeing yourself in context. Even leaders who are very independent work with others, and influence isn't only from the top down—it goes both ways. Great leaders recognize that they cannot just react; they need to think independently *and* have the humility to see how and upon whom they depend.

## Return to First Principles

A wise CEO once said to me, "Being in this job means being aware of multiples." When I asked Kevin what he meant, he said, "I need to think about strategy and keep a handle on operations, sales, finance, legal, our customers, owners, and the political climate. Since I can't do everything myself, I need to trust others. But I've learned not to be too dependent on them to be right about everything. I need to ask the right questions so that I can form an independent view."

Like many leaders, Kevin didn't achieve a perfect balance of independence and dependence, nor should anyone try. It's best to think of it like a light fixture on a rheostat (a dimmer switch). Sometimes more light is needed and at other times less is better—it depends on the circumstance. Kevin used this metaphor to help him decide when to dig in to something and when to back up. A marvelous side effect for him was that the image and his own discipline helped him feel less vulnerable.

Returning to first principles is a similar discipline, and anyone can practice it. The concept of first principles originated with Aristotle, who defined them as "the first basis from which a thing is known."[7] In mathematics and science, the implication of returning to first principles reduces the risk of building beautiful theories out of a deck of cards.

Whether consciously or not, great leaders are often suspicious of fads, bromides, and bandwagons, which is wise. At the same time, most leaders don't want to be a wet blanket, cynical of something merely because it's unfamiliar. Instead of being too dependent on how popular something is and investing in what could be a flashy bandwagon, and rather than rejecting it out of hand, a return to organizational first principles can help. A simple way to test whether you are too dependent or overly resistant to organizational habits, a trend, or a controlling person or people, and so on, is to use these questions to ground your discussions and thinking:

- Why does this organization exist?

- What value do we provide and to whom?

- If we proceed with this idea, how will it help us deliver what we promise?

- If we do not proceed, what opportunity to deliver what we promise are we missing?

Meta-leaders also use their position to guide the thinking of others back to first principles, from which intelligent people can make better decisions. In this way, a great leader is a thought leader who helps others cut through the noise and distraction to see what is real and important and to act accordingly.

## REFLECTING ON FACTORS THAT INFLUENCE OUR DECISIONS

The factors that affect your decisions will vary according to time and situation; how significant a single factor is will also vary. To better understand different factors that influence your decisions, ask questions such as these:

- How does my individual temperament play into the way I decide?

- How does my professional identity affect my response to situations?

- In what ways do my beliefs influence my decision-making?

- What habits of decision-making do I possess?

- How does my education affect the way I think about problems?

- What do I do first in a crisis?

# PART III

# BEHAVIOR

THINKING IS HOW we organize information, and emotion provides fuel, either to act or avoid doing so. Actions—subtle or overt, deliberate or habitual—are what lead to learning and change. Great leaders understand that actions, intentional or not, broadcast information to others about what is important, what is right, and what they should also do. They act deliberately on strategic issues and reflexively when facing matters of character—and they are conscious of the difference, recognizing that what they do has far more effect than what they say they will do.

# 7

# On Analysis
# and Synthesis

Analysis enables us to understand parts
of a whole and to see relationships
between different aspects of an organism,
organization, or phenomenon; it is taking apart
for examination. Synthesis enables insight
about the whole, without which analysis may be
technically correct but of little use.

I T WAS A COLD, clear day in Asheville, North Carolina, when I looked up at a beautiful blue sky, through trees whose leaves had turned brilliant yellow and orange. As I approached the steepest part of my walk, closer to the office, my joy began to turn to dread. Though I lived in a beautiful place and was happy in my personal life, I hated my job. This was a few short years into my tenure at the brokerage firm. I hadn't yet realized that I needed to pivot, but the events that were about to transpire would clarify that I was working in a position that was utterly wrong for me.

This day, it would turn out, would live in the annals of investing as a disaster. It was Monday, October 19, 1987. That day, the Dow Jones Industrial Average would fall by 508 points. Today, this doesn't sound as significant as it was then. However, at the time, it represented a 22.6 percent drop. A one-day decline this steep has, at the time of writing, not been eclipsed, thankfully.

Having been rattled by a drop of 108 points the Friday before, investors panicked. The *Philadelphia Inquirer* published this headline: "Dow Dives 508.32 Points in Panic on Wall Street." Newspapers worldwide reported the sell-off in the US and subsequent rattling of markets globally as panic ensued. Reporters identified various pressures that led to the terror, such as fear of rising interest rates, a bull market that had been running for five years without a significant correction, and increasing hostilities in the Persian Gulf.

No matter the reasons we identify post hoc, at the time emotion overtook investors—but not all of them. Over the next few weeks, as the aftershocks continued, I became riveted by the differences in the ways people responded. First, my boss, whom I called Mr. Big (before the *Sex and the City* writer used that moniker), showed zero empathy for our clients, who were understandably rattled. Next, one of the firm's clients who had a significant margin call (meaning he had borrowed money to purchase investments that were now worth substantially less, and he was obligated to pay back part of the debt) shot and killed the manager of one of the firm's offices, then shot and seriously wounded his broker, leaving him paralyzed, and finally, committed suicide. If that doesn't rattle you, nothing will.

Mr. Big locked the doors to our office and instructed us not to let in anyone we didn't know. Of course, I found that curious, since the client who had committed the mayhem wasn't a stranger. Nonetheless, we were behind closed doors for weeks, most of us—except for me—trying to act normal. I was taking it hard—not for myself, because I didn't have a lot of money and not much in the market at the time. Nevertheless, I was genuinely concerned that my clients might decide the stock market was nothing more than a giant roulette wheel and sell at the worst possible time. People commonly think of the value of investments as the same as that of cash, but, of course, they aren't equivalent. Gains and losses are realized only when the asset is sold.

What I noticed about people at that time has stayed with me ever since: even intelligent, knowledgeable, and experienced people fall into the trap of using either analysis or synthesis as a default. My technically inclined colleagues continued to stare at charts, while the fundamentalists simply reassured clients (and themselves), but without clear rationale.

I was, and remained for some time, haunted by how stuck most people were in their preferred methods, even if those methods were inadequate. The two-part question that I couldn't let go of then, and that continues to be the focus of my ongoing learning, musing, and advisory work today, is this: *Why isn't intelligence, knowledge, and experience a better predictor of good decision-making, and why, when we make a good decision, do we sometimes fail to act upon it?*

## Perfectly Bad Analysis and Beautifully Misguided Synthesis

In a crisis, such as the Wall Street meltdown of 1987, remaining calm enough to put things into long-term perspective is challenging, but that is what great leaders do. In typical sanguine style, Warren Buffett did not abandon his investment philosophy despite the chaos swirling around him. His strategy of buying shares in good companies at favorable prices has delivered steady returns for investors, neither stratospheric nor dismal, but reliable.

Leaders who are more susceptible to panic sometimes retreat into hyper-analysis, as some of my colleagues did. They put their heads down, studied charts, listened to the firm's experts, and dissected client holdings. But, of course, some of the analytics were neither valid nor reliable; instead, they were based on theories, to which various brokers had allegiance.

When feeling fear and threat of loss of status, some leaders engage in similar behavior, drilling down into details they wouldn't usually examine with such scrutiny. Sometimes a client will tell me that the board is "meddling," and this rarely occurs when results are excellent.[1] In the grip of black-and-white thinking, such as, "The board members are meddlers," people may not distinguish what is happening situationally from what is more general. When we are in the grip of any dichotomy, we may react in uncharacteristic ways. In the aftermath of the crash, our clients asked many questions they hadn't asked before. I wondered if some clients had always been very analytical and I was just noticing, or was their behavior understandable in the context of events? For most, it was the circumstances, but those who I understood to be very analytical increased their efforts, even though their work prior hadn't predicted the crash (very few people did).

Conversely, people sometimes leap to synthesizing by default, ignoring the value of analysis. Mr. Big was lightning-quick to judge, noticing only the most obvious factors and mashing them together. His opinions were strong, but nuance, logic, and accuracy weren't his strong suit. He believed that successful people were smart, well-dressed people were trustworthy, and if someone had a good vocabulary and was conversant in the language of business, they were worth his time. I didn't see his value, except as a figurehead. Although being mired in analysis can be paralyzing and indecisive, synthesis without any analysis might fly in the face of logic and accuracy.

Meta-leaders, however, use emotion as information. They use analysis to uncover critical information. Sometimes, the impetus to do so comes from synthesis—seeing a coherent story first—but using it as a jumping-off point rather than defending it.

## Our Faulty Data-Taking Devices (Aka the Five Senses)

The most straightforward explanation about why smart people make bad decisions is that humans are fallible. Neil deGrasse Tyson, an astrophysicist, director of the Hayden Planetarium at the American Museum of Natural History, and host of *StarTalk*, says, "Our five senses are faulty data-taking devices, and they need help."[2] It's true. What we perceive isn't simply a collection of our experiences. Instead, it is an amalgam that may bear little resemblance to another person's amalgam, which they believe is reality.

One reason our perceptions are not accurate recordings of things, people, and events is that there is simply too much stimulation for us to attend to everything. Humans simplify, categorize, and have preferred methods for doing so. Another reason we struggle to see reality is a phenomenon known as bounded rationality—certain cognitive limitations can prevent us from seeing a situation in full. Invisible to us, these unconscious limits nonetheless constrain our thinking. To work against bounded rationality, great leaders must accept that it is not only possible but likely that they will succumb to this trap, sometimes. If you are reading this and are annoyed by the mere idea that you have habits of thinking and making decisions that are sub-optimal, you are experiencing the effect of emotion on thinking. This happens to even the most intelligent people. For example, many organizations use self-referential benchmarking—comparing how they are doing against prior quarters, years, and so on. Some companies frequently survey customers and learn more and more about them while still knowing little about people who *aren't* customers but could be. Too often, strategic discussions are constrained by what is known rather than what could happen that is hard to imagine.

A hazard of expertise and experience is that they frequently come with a big side order of methodology and a particular approach to analysis. Methods of inquiry and analysis then confine our thinking. We forget that our methods are limited, mistaking analysis or synthesis for the royal road to truth. On my first day of graduate school, my professor, Dr. John DeCastro, told us a story that illuminates this point. It went like this: A man, Brad, walking along a sidewalk, sees another man, Fred, on his hands and knees under a streetlight, and stops to ask what he's doing. Fred says, "Looking for my keys."

Brad replies, "Did you drop them here?"

"No," says Fred. "I dropped them in that alley over there."

So Brad asks the logical question, "Why are you looking here?"

Fred's answer: "Because the light is better."

This story sounds simple and perhaps silly, but its point is important and worth reiterating. When faced with a difficult decision, such as where to direct our attention, we sometimes default to what is easier, even if it is ineffective. We use a means we know, even if it is not fitting to the circumstances. This is overgeneralization, meaning that we extend the use of something, in this case a technique, to circumstances where it does not apply.

What is more surprising is that sometimes we defend, even vociferously, decisions to use a particular tool when it doesn't work. It's doubtful that anyone would do this deliberately. Instead, the behavior results from a cognitive error. A person who only has a hammer sees a lot of nails. But when we have the hammer and see so many nails, we don't often realize that we see more nails *because* we know how to use a hammer. And wielding that hammer is easier than learning to use another tool (a circular saw, for example) that may do a better job for the task at hand (to cut a piece of plywood). The same applies to technical skills, interpersonal skills, and the like.

## How Identity Traps Us

Jason, a newly minted president of an $8 billion company, arrived precisely on time for our meeting. He was impeccably dressed, with slicked-back hair that looked as though it wouldn't move even in a strong wind. In the first five minutes, he said, "I'm analytical. People need to explain things to me in logical, provable terms." I asked him how his approach worked with his team. He said, "People are so frustrating. It's like they want a bedtime story, but the data *is* the story."

Jason was trapped by his extreme preference for analysis and hanging his professional identity on it. I declined to work with him. Why, you ask? He wanted me to change other people. That is not an objective I can work with. You may rightly imagine that Jason wasn't

**Even intelligent, knowledgeable, experienced people fall into the trap of using either analysis or synthesis as a default.**

———

in his role very long. Boards don't typically want to see a bunch of spreadsheets without a coherent narrative to go alongside, nor do they want to hear a beautiful story that isn't backed up by evidence. Great leaders want both data *and* description.

Conversely, consider a person like Bernie Madoff. Madoff was great at storytelling and astutely got others to do it for him. He had data all right, years of consistent returns, made possible by the influx of new money from investors, the very definition of a Ponzi scheme. And, as I discussed in Chapter 1, his investors were hardly witless dupes. Like Elizabeth Holmes of Theranos, Madoff used social proof, the concept identified and named by Robert Cialdini. People look to others to know how to act. I spoke with Cialdini about his work for my earlier book *High-Stakes Leadership* and was struck by how quickly he acknowledged that the ideas revealed by his research could be used for nefarious purposes.[3] This is what Madoff exploited. His investors' decision processes were interrupted by massive social proof.

When we know that people we respect have invested with someone, it lends tremendous credibility. Even if we don't know the people personally, we are influenced by the choices of others whom we wish to be like. Elizabeth Holmes garnered the support of world leaders like George Shultz and Henry Kissinger and other wealthy and sophisticated businesspeople who invested millions and lost it. When people we respect and believe to be similar to us in some critical way show support for an idea, business, or person, we are more likely to act based on our synthesis of the situation. Sometimes, when a person identifies as having a strong "BS detector," they accept more risk because deeper inquiry and analysis might mean their radar isn't so good.

## Myth Busters

People who follow Jim Cramer's advice to "buy and homework" are more likely to avoid several dangerous tendencies. First, when we are the buyer, we tend to think that the thing we are considering is worth less than the seller assumes. Real estate agents are very familiar with this, so they tell me. But, when selling, we tend to overvalue the investment, house, coin, stamp collection, and so on.

When I was a broker, some of my highly analytical clients bought investments only after considerable thought. Unfortunately, once they owned shares, they stopped being so attentive and analytical, meaning they did not want to hear new information or that something fundamental about the company had changed. Instead, they did what brokers refer to as "marrying" their investments. This is precisely what Cramer is trying to help us avoid: falling prey to the tendency to justify past decisions even if the facts have changed—and they always do.

Nathan is another myth buster. He was the head of human resources for a $35 billion global company in consumer products and newly in the role. As I watched Nathan take charge, I was impressed with his intellect and determination, even though he had a shortage of patience. I soon realized why he was so impatient.

At a meeting with his senior team, he listened to them present consolidated culture survey data as well as information from more than 8,000 360-degree feedback surveys. The headlines were: "Our employees love working here, and employees are well above average across the board." Nathan allowed the people presenting this information to finish, then asked, "Do you see anything wrong with this information?" Silence. He waited, then asked the question again. Nothing. Now visibly flushed and impatient, he said, "Let me ask you another question. What are our business results?" They were not remarkable, but the answer he got back was muted. Finally, he said,

"What you have presented may be numerical, but it is not what I call data. You have analyzed it up, down, and sideways, but you aren't seeing reality. If things are so great and everyone here is above average, then why is our business in trouble?"

Nathan went on to explain that good survey results aren't the goal. If they are positive but the company isn't doing well, then people either aren't seeing reality or aren't telling the truth. He was right. Accountability was low, and too many people were satisfied with achieving little. Nathan gave a master class in how data can be used to distort reality. Nathan, and great leaders like him, can provide the bridge between different approaches and methods. They are role models for integrating information rather than bifurcating it. They understand that using too little data, using invalid data, or failing to understand it in context will lead to a wrong decision.

In the case of Nathan, his first task was to see who on his team was willing to toss out what they thought they knew and who would defend the nice but inaccurate view of the company. He guided his team to do the following:

- Start with the end in mind. What does this organization do, for whom, and why?

- Define how the leadership team can, and should, contribute.

- Choose valid measures of success that answer the question, "How do we know if we are progressing?" Nathan insisted on linking what his team did to outcomes, rather than perfecting activity.

- Understand the limitations of various methods.

- Get to know the business and the people in it. Data is not a proxy for deep understanding, but it can tell you where to look.

## Fearless Curiosity

Leonardo da Vinci and Richard Feynman have some essential qualities in common, curiosity being among them. The sort of curiosity I refer to is not casual, though it may appear so, nor is it predictable based on a person's profession.

Da Vinci's interests ranged from painting to anatomy, engineering, and mathematics, to name a few. He followed his curiosity, sometimes to extremes in what we might call "going down rabbit holes," which we often utter with a tone of disdain. But da Vinci didn't restrict his interests to matters connected to his work as an artist. This provided him with valuable content, as he could see how seemingly unrelated objects, events, or fields of study applied to one another.

Walter Isaacson's biography of da Vinci is an incredible dive into the life and times of one of the world's greatest artists and thinkers. In the conclusion, Isaacson offers a series of lessons we can take from the life of da Vinci, some of which contradict what is espoused by many leaders. For example, a personal favorite from da Vinci is that we ought to "go down rabbit holes." Isaacson also cites "respect facts" and "take notes on paper."[4]

Feynman was deeply curious, and not just about physics. His joy in "finding out" extended to a quest to travel to Tuva and learn to play bongo drums. His dissatisfaction with answers that didn't make sense led him to conduct the simple experiment with an O-ring in a glass of ice water during the review of the *Challenger* explosion. Feynman was led by his desire to find out about all sorts of things, and like da Vinci, this gave him an incredible array of knowledge and experience on which to draw. While he was highly pragmatic, he was also willing to follow his curiosity and suspend the need to understand how doing so might be practical.

Sincere curiosity requires some courage, because when our interests don't converge or make sense to others, we may be on the receiving end of criticism. For example, my hobby is cooking and studying the history of culinary traditions, but I also like boxing. If I'm not in the mood to defend my interest in boxing, I don't talk about it. It makes no sense to almost anyone that I love something so domestic and also like a very physical sport (not as a participant, that's for sure). Cooking, that's excellent—very acceptable. According to most, the history of culinary traditions is a little less obvious but still okay. Boxing? How could I like it? It's so violent! Yes, it is, but because I was curious about it, I learned about it, and in doing so, I realized it isn't just about brute force. A great boxer makes decisions about each match. They analyze their opponent, then synthesize knowledge of their opponent and their strengths to develop a strategy.

## Museums, Movies, and Mysteries

Synthesis requires diverse content, the very thing that specialization makes less and less likely. Sometimes as people become more and more skilled at analysis, their breadth of knowledge constricts. Some people even narrow their fields of interest such that they eschew literature, art, theater, and international travel to any location other than the usual suspects. In contrast, great thinkers and meta-leaders possess breadth of knowledge but do not settle for mimicry; they seek understanding at a level that allows them to see similarities and distinctions and create useful analogies to convey profound meaning in few words.

Where do great leaders find this diverse content, and how do they choose? First, they tend to follow their interests, even if they are not typical. My long-time mentor, Alan Weiss, has an impressive setup of model trains, remarkable in both size and detail. He collects stamps, reads lots of fiction, and until recently was the board chair of the Providence Ballet. My friend and bestselling author Dorie Clark writes musicals, won a Grammy, and is known to have stayed up all night reading a thriller. Executives I advise enjoy deep-sea fishing, golf (one president of a public company has a 6 handicap!), and scuba diving, and all are readers. Weiss, Clark, and my clients have one very important attribute in common: they are observant. This enables them to learn from the most ordinary as well as extraordinary experiences.

Of course, it isn't possible to notice everything, and not everything we do note needs deep analysis. How do we decide? How can we create time and space for learning and thinking? The best way I know is to strategically delete what is in the way of our best selves and most laudable goals.

## ANALYSIS, SYNTHESIS, AND LEADERSHIP GROWTH

Here is a method to delete what isn't working and turn your attention, energy, and discipline toward rapid leadership growth:

1 Describe your ideal future self.

2 Define how you would spend your time, ideally, to become the self you have in mind.

3 Ask which tasks you do that are consistent with becoming who you wish to be and which are in the way. Delete the activities that are in the way.

4 Name four leaders you admire.

5 Identify the characteristics of the leaders you name.

6 Ask yourself which characteristics you share with those you admire, and amplify those.

8

# The Art of Knowing When to Act

Patience can be as courageous as action,

but it may appear as indecision.

Meta-leaders are aware of the pressure they

are under to be bold and act decisively,

but they use their well-developed sense of timing

to meet the needs of the circumstance.

**N**OT KNOWING can be intensely uncomfortable. When faced with a decision, leaders sometimes confuse what to do with when to do it.

John Leland was an amiable leader of a well-known and admired company that grew from a single location with less than thirty employees to a public company with more than 1,000 locations and more than 80,000 employees. Leland was a quiet, thoughtful man, so nondescript he often went unnoticed in a group. That is, until he spoke. Always prepared, relentlessly strategic in his thinking, and compassionate, he inspired trust.

Over many years, Leland assembled a team of leaders who possessed great skill but were utterly unlike him in appearance and demeanor. The partnership of steady, quiet leadership at the top and imposing leaders at the next level created uncommon loyalty among the employees, investors, and partners. I once asked a senior person, Joanne, why she had stayed with the company for more than fifteen years. She said, "Because of John Leland. He knows where we are going, what we're about, and makes sure we have what we need to do our best work." Joanne's comments were so striking that I've never forgotten them, and later I had the opportunity to share them with Leland. His response was entirely consistent with my view of him: he put his hands to his chest and said, "How wonderful to hear that. I will try to live up to that image; it is exactly what I aspire to be."

Sometime after this conversation, Leland was facing a succession challenge as he planned his retirement. A young, talented division president, Richard, was the obvious choice; however, I had doubts. Leland listened to my concerns but judged them to be less serious than I did. Fair enough. Maybe he was right, but Leland didn't want to sully his legacy with a succession fiasco. Senior leadership transitions are high-stakes decisions, but the outcomes aren't always immediately obvious. Leland didn't want to ignore even subtle signs that a possible successor was unfit.

But CEO transitions aren't only in the hands of the current CEO—at least they shouldn't be. The board of Leland's company, now valued at $30 billion, was very impressed with Richard because he had led his business unit from near bankruptcy to stellar results. The brand was energized and popular and had tremendous momentum, with same-store sales growing every quarter by double digits. On paper, Richard was perfect, and in person, impossible to ignore. Tall, perpetually tan, fit, impeccably and stylishly dressed, he was also engaging and articulate. He had a flair that was decidedly different from Leland's, a combination of cowboy and model. Indeed, he had an impressive collection of cowboy boots, always shined within an inch of their lives.

When Leland spoke with the board about wanting to test Richard a bit more, they didn't want to wait and pushed for a recommendation. One director expressed concern that Leland was postponing the decision because of ambivalence about his retirement. This is a fair question to ask, as CEOs who are retiring rather than moving to another CEO role can be extremely equivocal about timing and their successor. Retirement is a life event, not a job change, and it has a large psychological component that is almost always ignored, though it does rear its head, despite all efforts to contain the anxiety.

The board was suspicious that Leland's "later" stance was a sign that he may try to stay too long in his role without good reason. The board and Leland did agree to a one-year time frame, during which

Richard would take on a major strategic effort for the company. He was given an elevated title, but in a surprise move, another division president, Eloise, was also given a special role and new title. Eloise was happy to have the challenge of a new position. She hadn't expected to become CEO but saw an opportunity to lead on a larger stage. Eloise had been less strategic than Richard about her next career steps but was exceptionally competent and confident. Her calm assurance stood in stark contrast to the tension and impatience displayed by Richard. From his point of view, this was a horse race, and an unwelcome one.

Before I continue the story, let's deconstruct the situation from the point of view of dichotomous behavior. The board was determined to act right away, while Leland had a longer time frame. The board members

- realized it wouldn't be long before large shareholders and analysts would call the question;
- knew Leland was in his early sixties, and he needed to move on;
- thought Richard was fantastic, the obvious choice;
- understood that Richard was a public figure and that headhunters were probably swarming around him; and
- believed succession shouldn't take so much time, and that Leland was dragging his feet.

Leland also wanted to find his successor, but in that he

- understood this was a big decision and if they got it wrong, it could damage the company;
- knew his reputation was on the line;
- saw that Richard got great results but was a bit of a prima donna; and
- believed that a thorough process didn't mean he was dragging his feet.

Leland and the board of directors were in a dilemma by dichotomy—their perspectives were at extreme odds. They were playing tug-of-war over timing, each justifying their position with good reasons. People are often stuck in dichotomy dilemmas because they focus on the different approaches to a situation, rather than the objective. So, how to resolve it? In this case, the leaders could realize that the tension wasn't about timing at all—it was also about building confidence in the decision by taking the right actions. This is what happened.

First, the board and Leland affirmed their strategy and foreseeable challenges as well as the profile of what the ideal new leader would be like—their background, behavior, and attributes. This helped sidestep the problem of hiring a leader who looked good on paper but was hard to live with. Second, Richard and Eloise were each given clear objectives, some quantifiable but many qualitative and measured by observations of their behavior (not, however, by gossip, inference, or amateur psychoanalysis). Third, Leland and the board established a timeline, making it clear when a decision would be made, barring any events that would require action sooner.

As the board, Leland, and Eloise settled into the new arrangement, Richard became more impatient. A mere thirty days into the plan, he gave the board an ultimatum. He said, "Announce that I'm the next CEO or I'm taking another job."

Sadly, this behavior was Leland's worst nightmare: that Richard would (metaphorically) shoot himself in the cowboy boot. This sort of behavior is not uncommon in high-stakes situations like a CEO transition. As discussed in earlier chapters, emotion is an inseparable part of human thinking and behavior; it cannot be amputated no matter how intelligent a person may be. Richard's emotions, his need to be the top dog, got the better of him. But the board's reaction wasn't as immediate as you may think.

In the ensuing few days, chaos reigned in the boardroom, with some directors saying they should give Richard the nod, while others

We need goals and actions—but we do better when they're connected, and when our actions give us a glimpse of success.

were insulted and incensed by the ultimatum. The board decided that Richard's inability to tolerate their process was a harbinger of what it would be like to work with him as CEO. He left the company and took another CEO role, but unfortunately for this new organization, he took his anger and resentment with him. His worst attributes (smugness at the top of the list) were on full, and public, display. During his very short tenure at the new company, he encountered fierce opposition from virtually every group of stakeholders.

## The Long and the Short

As impatient a person as Richard could be, for most of his career he was playing a long game. Watching him lead was like watching someone play checkers with one hand and chess with the other. Richard could be demanding about short-term results so long as they were lined up with the long-term strategic objectives. He could see far into the future and notice the smallest details at the same time.

Richard mostly did what great leaders do. They have a big vision *and* they work to lay groundwork, build brands, innovate, and so on. They think and act with respect to now and later, making sure that what is done in the present is likely to lead to success later on.

Big goals almost always take time, but time alone doesn't get us there. Actions unconnected to our big goals are also insufficient. We need both goals and actions, but we do better when they are connected and when actions in the present give us a glimpse of success. Dorie Clark calls these "raindrops" and advises her clients to pay attention because they are small signs of being on the right track.[1] She advises her clients to recognize indications they are on the right track because ignoring them deprives people of a sense of achievement. Seeing the small signs is energizing, though they are often dismissed as unworthy of attention. Clark's book *The Long Game* bears witness to the wisdom of "now and later."

It's tough to be persistent when the fruits of our labor are long in coming. "I'll be happy when I have a million dollars," for example, or, "I'll be able to relax once I'm the CEO." Clark's advice—to set long-range objectives and pair them with the short-term actions most likely to get us there—describes precisely what great leaders do. The process of pairing short-term actions with objectives that take time to achieve is the same, though we sometimes ignore simple but profound ideas, resorting to habits that might not be in keeping with our objectives. Clark's idea—that we not only do the right things but also notice small signs of success along the way to a larger goal—is an important aspect of making changes in what we do permanent.

## Now or Never

Thousands of organizations establish advisory boards for all kinds of reasons, and sometimes in such a hurry that important questions remain unanswered. The time pressure seems very real because a good advisory board can help prevent mistakes that are hard to undo later. The urgency to do it now sometimes leads to an anxious sense that if not now, it will be never.

Leaders don't intentionally toss together an advisory board, but it happens in part because leaders look for experienced people and might assume they can figure out how to work together on the fly. However, that sets a tone that often continues to show up in meetings with agendas thrown together at the last minute. Soon, participating on a poorly run advisory board becomes an unwelcome obligation and the best people leave—either actively through resignation or passively by disengaging. It's a shame because a well-run advisory board is a source of value creation. Ironically, leaders who put together an advisory board precipitously may breathe a sigh of relief at having accomplished this task. But it will soon become evident that the talented and experienced people they recruited expect to be asked for advice now, not later. Leaders, especially those with less experience, have a wonderful opportunity to develop leadership skills, including those that will serve them well in their relationship with a governing board. If they already report to a board of directors or board of trustees, the advisors can help them strengthen their leadership skills as a peer to the board.

Advisory boards are merely the example here, but we can think of them like any team. Using Jon R. Katzenbach's definition, a team is "a small number of people with complementary skills who are committed to a common purpose, performance goals, and approach for which they hold themselves mutually accountable."[2] This framework is valuable for any group that seeks to work together to improve something.

Here are a few ideas to improve performance of an advisory board or other group meant to add value. These happen by intention, thought, investing in relationships, and taking a professional approach:

- **Create clarity of purpose.** When asked to join an advisory board, good leaders will inevitably ask, "What is the role of the advisory board for this organization?" Vague answers are a clue that the board is maintained out of habit rather than strategic intent. For example, if the purpose is to raise money, call it a donor development committee. Leaders who try to pass off a fundraising group as an advisory board may succeed, but the benefits will be temporary. One advisory board in healthcare education has a robust process, and the members are knowledgeable and well connected. They bring others into discussions of a strategic nature to benefit the specific organization and the future of healthcare more broadly. This organization provides an opportunity to give *and* derive satisfaction from so doing.

- **Build strong relationships.** Leaders who know the advisory board members beyond their LinkedIn profiles can call upon them for specific help. For example, Chris is a senior executive with deep experience in customer insight. When he joins a board of any type, Chris is frequently tapped to use his expertise to benefit the organization, which he finds very satisfying. However, while his expertise may be clear from his resume, what is not apparent on paper is his uncanny ability to turn data into a compelling story; that understanding of him only comes from investing in the relationship.

- **Bring your A game.** It is crucial to form and lead an advisory board as part of professional duties. If advisors realize that leaders have deprioritized this body or frequently excuse poor performance, it not only affects them but will reflect poorly on the organization.

The time to look at an advisory board, board of directors, or team is now and continuously. Regrettably, many groups defer such activities because they are "too busy" or think such actions are irrelevant. The pressures are understandable, but great leaders know that creating even small amounts of distance from habitual routines often yields insights that are priceless.

Leaders should ask themselves, "What is our objective for this advisory board?" If the answer is an outcome of high value, then it's worth treating it as a vehicle for value creation. Conversely, if it is not of high importance, or its purpose is more transactional, perhaps it's best not to have an advisory board at all. An advisory board can yield significant benefits when leaders sincerely work to articulate clarity of purpose, build relationships, and conduct themselves as professionally as they would other aspects of their role. If the objective for convening or continuing an advisory board is unclear or no longer valid, it's best not to have one. Meta-leaders are better than most at considering what to stop doing, which is at least as valuable as knowing what to do.

"Regret for the things we did can be tempered by time; it is regret for the things we did not do that is inconsolable."

———————

**SYDNEY J. HARRIS**

## Comfort Now, Regret Later

Journalist and author Sydney J. Harris's quote about regret—"Regret for the things we did can be tempered by time; it is regret for the things we did not do that is inconsolable"—is my all-time favorite quote.[3] It is a nudge, a provocative reminder that rumination changes nothing for the better. The list of things that leaders tell me they regret isn't long, but at the top is almost always, "I wish I hadn't waited so long to replace Neil." Here, with apologies to anyone who bears the name, "Neil" is a stand-in for any ineffective or destructive leader.

The second most common regret I hear is, "I wish I had dug into those numbers," with "those numbers" as a stand-in for anything slightly fishy. This regret is often associated with one of two things: an acquisition, merger, or partnership; or a suspiciously good result.

Why do intelligent people, especially leaders who we often think are hard-nosed, avoid unpleasantness? Because they are human. How do some people sidestep the trap of taking the easy way now when it makes a bigger mess later? They do the following:

- Reflect on mistakes and the context in which they happened
- Learn about their thinking and emotion, and how the context affects both

These ideas and others are beautifully explored in Daniel Pink's book *The Power of Regret*.[4] Pink's research includes the World Regret Survey, to which 19,000 people from 105 countries responded. When arranged into categories, regrets appear to be wide reaching. For example, some are regrets about career, education, relationships, and friendship. But the categories only tell us in what context people feel regretful, not why. It turns out that the number one regret is the regret of inaction, not doing something. Sydney Harris was right, but Daniel Pink gave us the proof.

Some of the examples that Pink provides are heart-wrenching because they are so personal. For example, some people look back with deep regret at having been a bully as a child, or at merely watching someone be bullied and doing nothing. Others had regret about not trying to build a relationship with someone they were attracted to, out of fear of rejection. The bigger surprise is how long-lasting regrets can be—decades long, it turns out.

One leader with whom I consulted, Kenneth, spoke about the regret of not removing his chief financial officer sooner. He promoted a very young, bright man to the role against the advice of the human resources leader and the board chairman. Kenneth, who prided himself on being a tough guy, wasn't about to back down. A former weight-lifting champion, he was an imposing figure and often reminded people that he wasn't afraid of anything. Of course, that wasn't true and never is. Fear is a necessary and important human emotion, but one that is pathologized along with regret.

Unfortunately, Kenneth was not only incapable of backing down, but he also couldn't admit error. Despite his belief that he was tough, he couldn't be tough-minded, especially with himself, and this weakness was the source of a striking vulnerability that led to numerous bad decisions. Ultimately, he was fired by a frustrated board of directors.

Whether born of stubbornness, arrogance, or something else, failures of action lead to many regrets. Yet, it is human to put things off in the belief we'll have time later. Sometimes that's true, but what if it isn't?

## HOW TO SOLVE A DILEMMA CAUSED BY DICHOTOMIZED THINKING

Precisely because dichotomous thinking is often automatic and outside of awareness, we see it only after the problems it has caused are evident. We needn't wait, though, until the entire scenario has played out. We can lean back at any time.

You can resolve to solve dilemmas by taking a meta-approach:

1   Develop your ability to observe yourself and more readily recognize when you are using black-and-white thinking. Warning: Knowing the concept of dichotomized thinking without devoting energy to seeing it in yourself can lead to thinking it's mostly other people who do this.

2   Find the words to describe the situation as a continuum, not a toggle. For example, a board might adopt a stance of "building the leadership bridge" to meet the need for leadership succession. However, sometimes and quite unwittingly, board members have biased and black-and-white thinking about future leaders. For example, the next CEO must have a particular background, education, or career path, or they either must be an insider or shouldn't be an insider.

3   Define the steps along the continuum or across the bridge.

4   Rethink the plan only if it proves to be based on assumptions later proven wrong.

# 9

# The Alchemy of Knowledge and Wisdom

Knowledge is the accumulation of information, facts, and experiences with a clear path to its attainment. How the insight and discernment that come with wisdom are achieved is more mysterious, almost magic.

ARRIE, A TALENTED and successful leader in a pharmaceutical company, furrowed her brow and, in an irritated voice, said to me, "Why do you keep telling me that the people I think are smart are average?" She routinely made a common mistake, using knowledge and vocabulary as a proxy for capability. We'd had this discussion in the past, but Carrie initially didn't have a lot of patience for my observations. She preferred quick answers and actionable advice. Still, she was curious enough to realize I might be able to help her see something that others were missing.

Carrie was a bright woman with deep experience in her industry, but she fell into habits that were not serving her, or her organization, well. First, she was overusing what she already knew, even when faced with multiple mistakes. She showed impatience with learning unless the topic was straightforward and technical. When it came to human behavior, she resorted to personality types or popular bromides. As articulate as she was, she could be surprisingly shallow.

Because Carrie's employer was attractive, she met many applicants with industry experience. In interviews, she and her colleagues were often impressed by the applicants' knowledge but didn't realize they were also distracted by it. Carrie began to see the downside of overusing knowledge when many of the people she hired, whom she believed were intelligent, failed. She knew she needed to adopt a more nuanced way to think about the characteristics she was looking for. But before she had built a stronger ability to assess people, Steve showed up.

Steve arrived with an impressive resume to interview for an executive role. He impressed Carrie with his industry fluency, connections, and track record. Steve wore starched shirts complete with a monogram on the cuffs. He was a high-energy fast talker with a jocular manner. Carrie was ready to hire him until she remembered her commitment to be more deliberate, more comprehensive, and less willing to give in to her need for speed. Realizing her tendency to short-circuit the hiring process if the person demonstrated deep knowledge (she named this the "knowledge trap"), she put the brakes on. To Carrie's surprise, her colleagues pushed back. Carrie had a deserved reputation for making rapid decisions, and the change in her behavior made others nervous. Her team was pushing to fill the executive position and made no secret of their impatience. Finally, Carrie gave in to the pressure, in part because she realized it was she who had reinforced the group's tendency to hire for knowledge, do it fast, and deal with higher than desirable turnover as an unavoidable consequence.

Unfortunately, in the two years that Steve was with the company, he hired and fired an astonishing number of sales leaders, insulted some key customers, and hid problems from Carrie. He not only tarnished his own reputation, but he made Carrie look bad. Fortunately for Carrie, her colleagues rallied around her and admitted they hadn't been as diligent as necessary.

Over the following year and half, Carrie and her team worked to become better at selecting new colleagues and promoting for the right reasons. They could see that while knowledge is essential, senior leaders also need to have intelligence, insight, and good judgment. The team learned, together, that they unwittingly placed too much emphasis on speed and were impressed by confidence even if it was unearned.

## The Path to Wisdom

The task before Carrie was more complicated than it may appear and is not achieved by rigid technique. She said, "I need better skill in interviewing, but what I really need is wisdom." In a recent conversation, she reflected on the ten years we have known each other and her growth as a leader. This is what she said:

> At least in my mind, I was a hotshot and thought I knew almost everything I needed to know. Unfortunately, my arrogance prevented me from learning and prevented others from trying to help me. I hired people I thought were brilliant, but I was hiring people like me, articulate but over-reliant on good communication skills. I pushed aside anyone outside my industry and looked down my nose at anyone who didn't have at least an MBA. Now I understand that to be a wise leader, I need to know as much as possible, *but I can't learn if I think I already know.*

Carrie is now on the precipice of her next leadership role. Though it is a few years out, she is already thinking about what she will need to learn and with whom she needs to form relationships. She knows that mistakes will happen, but they are rarely fatal, and admitting error is a sign of a good leader, not a stain. Carrie also knows that learning never ends. She has abandoned her tendency to prove that she is the most knowledgeable person in the room. She practices my "learn in public" method, allowing people with expertise to teach her what they know in the presence of other people. She is becoming a wise leader.

## Redemption through Reflection

Carrie had fallen into very human tendencies to use default think-ing. Looking back, she realized that she used dichotomies to control others and keep the upper hand in discussions. Using her distinc-tive voice, volume, and intense gaze, she would frame decisions and options as "this or that" with such intensity that few opposed her. She wasn't interested in nuance or multi-factorial causes, which, unfortunately, meant that she made mistakes and didn't allow oth-ers to help her avoid error. It took a series of very disruptive events for Carrie to look at herself rather than at others as the cause of problems. That said, she has become skilled at facing problems and mistakes head-on, looking for cause more than blame.

Although a retrospective may be helpful, looking for blame is easier than pinpointing cause. Investigations often prioritize knowledge—who did what, when, how, and so on—but under-standing cause requires a more holistic approach. Sometimes investigations of wrongdoing lead to punishment but no improve-ment, because the leaders are trying to settle matters quickly and show others that they "took decisive action."

Recall the ignition switch disaster at General Motors we discussed in Chapter 5. When she assumed the position of CEO, Mary Barra could have settled for knowing "who did it" and punishing them. Of course, knowing who the bad actors were was essential, but her inquiry sought more than knowledge. She was after wisdom: What circumstances made it suitable for people who knew to keep quiet?

## Wise Leaders Use the Right Knowledge

Simplifying is necessary, lest we drown in detail and remain para-lyzed over straightforward decisions. Deciding what flavor of ice cream to buy can be more fun when done impulsively, and the

# Great leaders use wisdom to help them discern what knowledge is needed in what circumstance.

———————

downside of choosing a flavor we don't like is negligible. Most people give a wide berth to someone who stands in the ice cream shop and pontificates about the fat content or origin of ingredients.

The ice cream example is extreme and ridiculously obvious. Unfortunately, the same behavior in another context can be harder to recognize, except in hindsight. The reason is entirely down to context.

Imagine you are in a room with a chief marketing officer and her team, who are reporting the results of recent changes to the company website and a social media campaign. The first person reports data about engagement with the website, and the next speaks about "likes" on LinkedIn and Twitter, each subtly (or not) trying to paint the best picture of their efforts. Their data says they are great and their teams are fantastic. Success!

The team members finish their presentations, sit back, and wait for the CMO to tell them how well they are all doing. But that doesn't happen. Instead, she asks what it all means. The company's sales are lagging and no one is sure why. She's asking, "What insights can we glean about our customers and the marketplace where potential customers hang out?" The CMO is looking at the data *in relation* to other indicators. Unfortunately, her team hadn't tied what they were working on to the type of information the CMO and her boss, the CEO, need. It is not an uncommon trap—a measure of one thing unwittingly becomes a proxy for the thing itself. It's a case of FOTWT (fot-wit): focusing on the wrong thing.

The problem with FOTWT is it causes tunnel vision but at the same time can make us feel knowledgeable. Call centers that evaluate employees based on how quickly they handle calls commit this crime against good service. If you've ever called Apple or Zappos, you can bet they aren't measuring quality by time. How can I tell? They do several things extremely well. First, they listen to understand what your problem is. Second, they reassure you that they will help.

Third, they walk you through the possible remedies. Fourth, they stay on the call until the issue is resolved or until a next step is identified.

Consultants can be extremely hard-headed about measures of success, focusing on terrible indicators such as the number of networking events attended, number of "likes" of a tweet or post, number of hours worked, and so on. If the goal is to grow a business, better outcome measures are revenue, margin, market share, and the like. Yet, brilliant people who embark on consulting careers have argued with me, vociferously, that their CRM systems must be set up before they can do any marketing, for example.

Focusing on the wrong thing may be an honest mistake imposed by a system we don't control. It can also be an avoidance tactic, keeping us from doing the work most likely to help us achieve our goals. Knowing everything there is to know about websites, if that isn't your business, may alleviate some fear, but it isn't wise.

Great leaders use wisdom to help them discern what knowledge is needed in what circumstance. They don't settle for "more is better," nor are they swept away by fads, bandwagons, and bumper-sticker advice. Importantly, great leaders don't make decisions about hiring employees or consultants according to experience alone. Wise leaders know that experience doesn't necessarily make a person smart. Sometimes experience makes people rigid.

## Cultivating Wisdom

Great leaders help others develop wisdom by guiding them to reflect on past decisions, attending to thinking, emotion, and behavior. The adage about learning from mistakes may be true, but learning from success can be even more important. Studying mistakes can show us what *not* to do, but it can leave a vacuum. Knowing what makes us great shows us what to perpetuate, augment, and teach others.

"Yesterday I was clever, so I wanted to change the world. Today I am wise, so I am changing myself."

———

**RUMI**

Deconstructing mistakes and success is vital to learning. It leads to:

- more acute awareness of our thought processes;
- understanding the force of organizational culture on our behavior;
- recalling pressure or support we received and from whom;
- recognizing our tendencies to step into decision traps and to which of these we are most vulnerable;
- accepting that we need the talents and knowledge of others to help us;
- seeing the recurrent barriers so we can move them out of the way; and
- unearthing assumptions that weren't obvious earlier.

Deconstruction is the act of taking something apart while retaining the component parts. *It is not demolition*, which changes the elements. For example, a group of leaders working to understand why their acquisition of a company was successful might consider these elements:

- Business model
- Leadership
- Customers
- Employees
- Financial terms
- Market conditions and trends
- Organizational culture
- Opportunities
- Headwinds

These elements don't exist independently, and deconstructing helps us more readily see the parts of a system along with what may have been obscured. Further, upon reflection it is easier to ask, "What element of luck or happenstance was helpful?" and "What bad luck did we have?" This very real and critical part of any business is easy to ignore because it is completely out of our control.

Who knew that the global pandemic that began in 2020 would happen when and in the way it did? Yet more mundane winds of fortune and misfortune can also help or harm a business. Top leaders leave or become ill, suppliers have a disaster, technology fails, weather stops commerce in its tracks, labor strikes or shortages disrupt the market, and so on. As valuable as deconstruction of what is, or of what has already happened, can be, it can also be done *as a future exercise* that informs, helps leaders create, and illuminates risk. In this way, it helps leaders use knowledge and wisdom, while expanding both.

## Untangling Wisdom from Mythology

Still, the dichotomy of knowledge and wisdom has particular tension because wisdom is a positive ideal that people tend to claim less often than other qualities, such as courage. The paths to knowledge are multiple and seemingly more obvious, while becoming wise can be mysterious, perhaps requiring a bit of magic. Wisdom can seem unattainable, and the very idea of seeking it inspires a sense that we may be unrealistic and reach too far.

If we can untangle wisdom from mythology, we can learn how to marry knowledge and wisdom. Letting go of the idealized notion that wise men and women are smart about everything is a start. Instead, we can look for when and where we are wise. We can acknowledge others for their wise judgments as well as for what they know. No matter how little wisdom we think we possess, it can be cultivated—starting right now. These questions can serve as a guide:

- What are the gifts that I bring?
- What do I want others to say about my contributions?
- Am I enthusiastic about learning?

- Am I able to remain calm (or calm myself) in a crisis?
- Do others seek my advice?
- Do I provide insight on thorny issues?
- Am I able to synthesize and summarize complex issues?
- Am I more curious than judgmental toward others?
- Finally, do I inspire people to use their talents for a common purpose?

Wise leaders are knowledgeable *and* aware of the environment, other people, and the power of culture. Most of all, intelligent leaders understand themselves and use their talents to move others toward laudable goals.

Wise leaders, meta-leaders, see dichotomies and say, "Yes, both can be true, and sometimes at the same time."

## FOCUS ON THE RIGHT THINGS

Wise leaders focus on what matters most and bring their knowledge to bear on what has the greatest impact. Here are some questions to help you identify what matters most and do them well, and to abandon the things that take resources but matter little or not at all:

- What do we want to be different in a year?

- How will we know if we are successful?

- If we succeed, for whom will it matter and how?

- If we fail, what are the likely reasons?

# Acknowledgments

I OWE A great deal to the many senior executives with whom I have worked and from whom I have learned the realities of leadership at the highest levels. The boards of directors and trustees who have sought my advice and counsel in high-stakes, confidential decisions have shown me what good governance looks like in action and what striving to improve it requires of board leaders.

Dr. Pamela Fox, president of Mary Baldwin University (MBU) in Staunton, Virginia. Dr. Fox has ably led the evolution of MBU to serve a diverse population of students, helping many earn an education that improves their own lives and that of their families and communities. During her presidency (2003–2023), Dr. Fox led MBU to expand who it serves and how. MBU stands as an example of meta-leadership, thanks in great part to her work.

Dr. Timothy (Tim) Renick, whom I refer to in the introduction of this book. In his work to change the success rate of undergraduates at Georgia State University to one rightly admired by universities around the world, he embodies meta-leadership.

Dr. James (Jim) Detert, John L. Colley Professor of Business Administration at Darden School of Business at the University of Virginia, for his research on courage, to which I refer almost daily.

Dr. Frances Frei, professor of technology and operations management at Harvard Business School, for her research and ability to communicate what she knows.

Dorie Clark, for always putting her finger on the most important ideas I create and pushing me to use them.

Mark Levy, the master of taking my unformed ideas and expressing them in a few well-chosen words.

Lorraine Moore and Drs. Linda Henman, Joanne Irving, Richard Citrin, and Helen Turnbull, peers whom I admire, whose advice I seek and respect, and without whom my life would be far less rich.

The leaders, scientists, writers, artists, and great thinkers from whom I have learned so much, some in person, others from their writing and public appearances:

| | | |
|---|---|---|
| Madeleine Albright | David Eagleman | Toni Morrison |
| Jacinda Ardern | Richard Feynman | Jacqueline Novogratz |
| Margaret Atwood | Walter Isaacson | Richard Thaler |
| Lisa Feldman Barrett | Daniel Kahneman | Howard Thurman |
| Heather Berlin | Anne Lamott | Neil deGrasse Tyson |

# Notes

**Introduction**

1   Korzybski, A. (1933). *Science and sanity: An introduction to non-Aristotelian systems and general semantics*. International Non-Aristotelian Library Publishing Company, p. 58.

2   Renick, T. (n.d.). *Teaching statement*. Georgia State University. Retrieved June 29, 2022, from usg.edu/faculty_affairs/assets/faculty_affairs/documents/awards02_trenick.pdf.

3   National Institute for Student Success. (2021, March 20). *The mission* [Video]. YouTube. youtube.com/watch?v=bc6N15vmvOo.

4   Gumbel, A. (2020). *Won't lose this dream: How an upstart urban university rewrote the rules of a broken system*. New Press.

5   Renick, T. (2022, January). Personal communication.

**1: A Certain Discomfort with Uncertainty**

1   Keats, J. (1925). *Letters of John Keats to his family and friends* (S. Colvin, Ed.). Macmillan and Co., p. 48.

2   Abed, R. (2019, March 29). Billionaire Charlie Munger says admitting failure is key to success. Here are 5 ways to embrace failure. *Inc.* inc.com/robbie-abed/want-happiness-success-take-this-simple-advice-from-warren-buffetts-right-hand-man.html.

3   Lam, J. (2014). *Enterprise risk management: From incentives to controls*. Wiley.

4   James, E.H., & Wooten, L.P. (2022). *The prepared leader: Emerge from any crisis more resilient than before*. Wharton School Press, p. 64.

5   Cohen, P. (2011, November 30). A gallery that helped create the American art world closes shop after 165 years. *New York Times*. nytimes.com/2011/12/01/arts/design/knoedler-art-gallery-in-nyc-closes-after-165-years.html;

Moynihan, C. (2016, February 10). Knoedler Gallery and collectors settle case over fake Rothko. *New York Times*. nytimes.com/2016/02/11/arts/design/knoedler-gallery-and-collectors-settle-case-over-fake-rothko.html.

6   Avrich, B. (Director). (2020). *Made you look: A true story about fake art* [Film]. Documentary Channel Original.

7   Tversky, A., & Kahneman, D. (1974). Judgment under uncertainty: Heuristics and biases. *Science*, 185(4157), 1124–31. doi.org/10.1126/science.185.4157.1124.

8   Shermer, M. (n.d.). The measure of a woman: An interview with social scientist Carol Tavris. *Skeptic*. Retrieved June 29, 2022, from skeptic.com/eskeptic/11-02-09/#feature.

### 2: The Most Rational among Us Can Be Irrational

1   Cialdini, R.B. (1993). *Influence: The psychology of persuasion* (Revised ed.). William Morrow, p. 116.

2   Eisen, B. (2020, February 21). Wells Fargo reaches settlement with government over fake-accounts scandal. *Wall Street Journal*. wsj.com/articles/wells-fargo-nears-settlement-with-government-over-fake-account-scandal-11582299041.

### 3: Strategy and Tactics Move the Needle

1   Martin, R.L. (2014, January–February). The big lie of strategic planning. *Harvard Business Review*. hbr.org/2014/01/the-big-lie-of-strategic-planning.

2   Gunther McGrath, R. [@rgmcgrath]. (2021, November 22). *Most strategic planning exercises are budgeting in a Halloween costume!* [Tweet]. Twitter. twitter.com/rgmcgrath/status/1462856113150431233.

3   Lam. *Enterprise risk management*.

4   Baron, J., & Hershey, J.C. (1988). Outcome bias in decision evaluation. *Journal of Personality and Social Psychology*, 54(4), 569–79. doi.org/10.1037/0022-3514.54.4.569; Mazzocco, P.J., Alicke, M.D., & Davis, T.L. (2004). On the robustness of outcome bias: No constraint by prior culpability. *Basic and Applied Social Psychology*, 26(2–3), 131–46. doi.org/10.1080/01973533.2004.9646401.

### 4: To Be Analytical or to Be Creative Is Not Destiny

1   Birsel, A. (2015). *Design the life you love: A step-by-step guide to building a meaningful future*. Ten Speed Press.

2   Eagleman, D. (2020). *Livewired: The inside story of the ever-changing brain*. Pantheon Books.

3   Kahneman, D. (2011) *Thinking, fast and slow*. Farrar, Straus and Giroux, p. 85.

4   Fendt, J. (2006). CEOs and managerialism, success trap, blind trust, and global mindset: Introducing the individual vigilance/social experimentation framework. *Journal of Business and Economic Research*, 4(12). doi.org/10.19030/jber.v4i12.2719.

5   Keynes, J.M. (1936). *The general theory of employment, interest, and money.* Macmillan and Co., p. viii.

6   Irving, J. (2022, January). Personal communication.

7   Feynman, R. (1999). Cargo cult science: The 1974 Caltech commencement address. In *The pleasure of finding things out: The best short works of Richard P. Feynman* (J. Robbins, Ed.). Perseus, p. 212.

### 5: The Fallacy of Absolute Courage and Total Cowardice

1   Norton, J.D. (2016). How Einstein did not discover. *Physics in Perspective*, 18, 249–82. doi.org/10.1007/s00016-016-0186-z.

2   Detert, J. (2021). *Choosing courage: The everyday guide to being brave at work.* Harvard Business Review Press.

3   Fellowes, J. (Writer) & Goddard, A. (Director). (2012, January 15). Season 2, Episode 3 [TV series episode]; Fellowes, J. (Writer) & Morshead, C. (Director). (2015, January 18). Season 5, Episode 3 [TV series episode]. In Fellowes, J. (Writer & Creator), *Downton Abbey.* Carnival Films.

4   Frei, F., & Morriss, A. (2012). *Uncommon service: How to win by putting customers at the core of your business.* Harvard Business Review Press; Frei, F. (2018, April). *How to build (and rebuild) trust* [Video]. TED Conferences. ted.com/talks/frances_frei_how_to_build_and_rebuild_trust?language=en.

5   Frei, F. (2019, May). Personal communication.

6   Glazer, E. (2016, September 16). How Wells Fargo's high-pressure sales culture spiraled out of control. *Wall Street Journal.* wsj.com/articles/how-wells-fargos-high-pressure-sales-culture-spiraled-out-of-control-1474053044.

7   Peck, M.S., quoted in Detert. *Choosing courage*, p. 78.

8   Edmondson, A.C. (2019). *The fearless organization: Creating psychological safety in the workplace for learning, innovation, and growth.* Wiley.

9   Campbell, J. (2008). *The hero with a thousand faces* (3rd ed.). New World Library.

### 6: Independent Decisions Always Depend On Something

1   Konnikova, M. (2016). *The confidence game: Why we fall for it . . . every time.* Penguin Books.

2   Kahneman. *Thinking, fast and slow*, p. 31.

3   Tomky, N. (2021, July 12). Here are the most popular ice cream flavors in every state, according to Instacart. *Kitchn.* thekitchn.com/most-popular-ice-cream-flavors-instacart-23200237.

4   Feynman, R. (1988). *"What do you care what other people think?" Further adventures of a curious character.* W.W. Norton & Company.

5   Presidential Commission on the Space Shuttle *Challenger* Accident. (1986). V: The contributing cause of the accident. In *Report of the Presidential Commission on the Space Shuttle* Challenger *Accident* (Vol. 1). history.nasa.gov/rogersrep/genindex.htm.

6    Feynman, R.P. (1986). Appendix F: Personal observations on reliability of shuttle. In *Report of the Presidential Commission on the Space Shuttle* Challenger *Accident* (Vol. 2). history.nasa.gov/rogersrep/v2appf.htm.

7    Irwin, T. (1989). *Aristotle's first principles.* Oxford University Press.

### 7: On Analysis and Synthesis

1    Dierickx, C. (2019, July 18). What senior executives can do when the board meddles. *Harvard Business Review* hbr.org/2019/07/what-senior-executives-can-do-when-the-board-meddles.

2    deGrasse Tyson, N. (2009, July 21). Panel discussion. Center for Inquiry, New York Academy of Sciences.

3    Dierickx, C. (2017). *High-stakes leadership: Leading through crisis with courage, judgment, and fortitude.* Bibliomotion.

4    Isaacson, W. (2017). *Leonardo da Vinci.* Simon & Schuster, pp. 521, 524.

### 8: The Art of Knowing When to Act

1    Clark, D. (2021). *The long game: How to be a long-term thinker in a short-term world.* Harvard Business Review Press.

2    Katzenbach, J.R., & Smith, D.K. (2005, July–August). The discipline of teams. *Harvard Business Review.* hbr.org/2005/07/the-discipline-of-teams.

3    Harris, S.J. (1951, January 5). Syd cannot stand Christmas neckties. *Akron Beacon Journal*, p. 6.

4    Pink, D.H. (2002). *The power of regret: How looking backward moves us forward.* Riverhead Books.

# Index

# About the Author

CONSTANCE DIERICKX, PhD, is an author, speaker, and consultant who works with boards and senior executives in the US and internationally, specializing in crisis intervention and high-stakes decision-making. Her acclaimed previous books are *High-Stakes Leadership: Leading through Crisis with Courage, Judgment, and Fortitude* (2017) and *The Merger Mindset: How to Get It Right in the High-Stakes World of Mergers, Acquisitions, and Divestitures*, co-authored with Linda Henman, PhD (2018). In 2021, she was named Consultant of the Year by the Society for the Advancement of Consulting. Dierickx has been interviewed for publications such as the *Wall Street Journal, Fast Company, Directorship*, and Fortune.com. She has written for a wide number of publications, including *Forbes, Harvard Business Review, Directors & Boards, Chief Executive*, and *Corporate Board Member*.

Dierickx earned her PhD in clinical psychology from Georgia State University. She lives in Atlanta.

# Master the Art of Meta-Leadership

**T**HE IDEAS presented in this book can be useful for anyone, CEOs included. I hope you see examples of meta-leaders in your everyday life, and perhaps now you'll recognize aspects of meta-leadership in others and, very importantly, in yourself.

The idea is simple. Use your mind to consciously observe your thinking, emotions, and behavior, and use a mental rheostat to adjust the angle and altitude to help you see what others don't and make great decisions.

A series of questions you can ask to help implement these ideas and develop your own rheostat can be found at:

constancedierickx.com/resources

### Move from a simple idea to practice: how to get in touch

My work helps leaders use ideas like meta-leadership in real time and actual situations. Leaders don't reach out, at least to me, because I have a bright shiny object to offer. Leaders work with me on what is really happening in their business, organization, or institution. They want to be sure they are seeing what is really happening, thinking about it as clearly as they can, and avoiding traps along the way.

If you want to discuss your situation, reach out to me:

constance@constancedierickx.com

### Spread the idea of meta-leadership and why it matters

If you want others in your organization to learn about the ideas in this book and you don't want to tell them yourself, I can help.

If you are interested in having me speak to your leadership group, you will find information at constancedierickx.com/speaking.

## Share the love

Many great leaders like to share ideas in book form with their teams—and sometimes their families! *Meta-Leadership* is available at your favorite bookstore, of course. If you wish to purchase more than 25 copies, my fantastic publishing partners at Page Two can assist and will make it easy. Contact them at orders@pagetwo.com. Orders of 100 copies or more will receive a discount.

## Find more from me here

constancedierickx.com/blog

### Articles on *Harvard Business Review* blog

"What Senior Executives Can Do When the Board Meddles": hbr.org/2019/07/what-senior-executives-can-do-when-the-board-meddles

"Why New Leaders Should Make Decisions Slowly": hbr.org/2019/09/why-new-leaders-should-make-decisions-slowly

"Returning to the Office Will Be Hard. Here's How Managers Can Make It Easier.": hbr.org/2021/08/returning-to-the-office-will-be-hard-heres-how-managers-can-make-it-easier

### *Marketplace Morning* on National Public Radio

"How Can Company Leaders Best Manage a Return to the Workplace?": marketplace.org/2021/09/15/how-can-company-leaders-best-manage-a-return-to-the-workplace

### Articles at Forbes.com

forbes.com/sites/constancedierickx